How To Turn Your Money Life Around

The Money Book For Women

RUTH L. HAYDEN

Health Communications, Inc.
Deerfield Beach, Florida

Library of Congress Cataloging-in-Publication Data

Hayden, Ruth L.
   How To Turn Your Money Life Around: The Money Book
   For Women/Ruth L. Hayden.
     p.   cm.
   Includes bibliographical references.
   ISBN 1-55874-225-5
   1. Women — Finance, Personal.   I. Title
HG179.H346   1992
332.024 042 — dc20   92-2972
                                           CIP

© 1992 Ruth L. Hayden
ISBN 1-55874-225-5

Publisher: Health Communications, Inc.
             3201 S.W. 15th Street
             Deerfield Beach, FL 33442-8190

Cover design by Robert Cannata

🪱 CONTENTS

Part I • What Did I Learn?

1. What's The Matter With Me? 3
2. How Did I Get This Way? 13
3. Why Is Money So Hard For Me? 23
4. No Matter What I Do, It Doesn't Work 37

Part II • Unlearning The Learning

5. No More! 51
6. It's My Life. I Get To Decide 59
7. Someday Is Here 73
8. This Is A Budget? 83
9. I'm In Charge. Yes, I Am 99
10. It's Working! 121

Epilogue: What Do I Do Next? 137

Appendix: Resources And Bibliography 143

🜊 INTRODUCTION

> **First you change your attitude.**
> **Then you change your life.**

This book is for women who have tried to make changes in their personal finances and have failed. They've tried to figure out why these changes haven't worked and why they end up feeling out of control, undisciplined and discouraged. They may be in emotional pain. They may be in financial crisis. Whatever the problems, they know for sure that whatever they are doing, it isn't working. They don't know what caused these money problems and don't know how to fix these problems. They just know they are tired of feeling and acting this way with their money.

This book is for women who have decided *not* to passively accept their discouragement, their pain, their crises and their frustration with money. It is for women who want to understand why they have a problem with money and what they can do to rid themselves of this problem in their money lives.

This book is divided into two sections:

The first section explores the early training you had about money and looks into the emotional and financial consequences of that training. Analyzing the consequences of your money training will help you motivate yourself to change your money life. Part I helps you to say, "I *must* change."

The second part asks you to decide what you are willing to do to change the learning you identified in Part I in order to learn new ways to work with money in your life. This section teaches you new money skills that will help you change your money life. Part II helps you to say, "I *can* change."

This book is based on the "Women and Money" classes I have taught for nine years. As you work through this book, picture yourself as one of the 14 women in the "Women and Money" class. You, like the rest of the women, are reading and writing and talking.

Like the women in the class, you may want to have available a notebook so you can take notes and work through the assignments. *This notebook will become a record of your personal journey of financial empowerment.* A very large eraser and a small calculator will also be useful.

This book, like the classes, has three change-places. These are three places where you will be asked to make attitudinal and financial pivots.

You are at the first pivot *right now:* You have picked up this book. You may be feeling denial or hopelessness or anger or shame or frustration or confusion, or you may be rationalizing and blaming. All these emotions are part of the powerlessness of your financial learning. "There seems to be a bit of a problem with me and my money" is the first attitudinal pivot. This pivot will take you right through Part I.

The second change-place is a decision pivot. This pivot is the decision to move out of your hopelessness, frustration and victim stance into letting go and acceptance. The language of this pivot is, "Okay, I'm going to do it. No more of the old powerlessness. It's time to move forward into growth." Chapter 5 is the decision pivot. It is a small chapter, yet it carries the weight of the book on it. This chapter asks you to make a decision to move away from powerlessness and toward financial empowerment.

The language of the third change-place is, "I'm ready to change. But *how* do I make these attitudinal and financial changes?" All it takes to develop these attitudinal and financial changes is clarity, planning and practice, practice, practice and more practice. Chapters 6, 7, 8, 9 and 10 will teach you the *how* of new attitudinal and financial skills.

Everyone needs a teacher when learning a new skill. A teacher helps you learn the new skills, gives you support and holds you accountable. Please let me be your teacher. As your teacher, I know you can learn these new skills. And, as your teacher, I can show you how.

Many, many women have used this method to make changes in the way they think about money and the way they act with their money.

Now, if you choose, you can too.

Positive Attitude + Financial Change = Successful Living

DEDICATION

To my partner and friend,
The one I share my life with . . .

For all your love and support.

ACKNOWLEDGMENTS

I would like to thank Peter Vegso, Barbara Nichols, Lisa Moro and Teri Miller at Health Communications for working with me and with this book in a manner of the highest professionalism and respect. Most of all, I would like to thank my editor, Marie Stilkind, for her enthusiasm, her support and for her fine professional skills.

I would like to thank the women in my life who have supported the writing of this book with their editing help and with their emotional support.

I would like to thank Don and our children, Jenny, Steven, Nate and Christina for their support and their patience.

And, finally, I would like to thank all the women who have been in the "Women and Money" classes, willing to share with the other women in the classes and with me. Without this learning and sharing, this book would never have been. Thank you — all of you. It has been a privilege to know you.

PART I

WHAT
DID I LEARN?

❧ ONE ☙

WHAT'S THE MATTER
WITH ME?

I never have any money left at the end of the month. I always just barely make it.

Vickie

Every time I put money in a savings account, I have to take it back out to pay bills or buy groceries.

Kathryn

Each month my charge accounts get bigger and bigger, and I can't figure out what I bought that cost so much.

Pam

I'm tired and discouraged. I'm always in some crisis about money. Being in crisis reminds me how alone I am and how unlovable I feel. I don't know if things can ever be any different. I don't know what to do.

Jennifer

I've always wanted to have my own home, and I don't think I'll ever get it.

Anne

I'm afraid I'll become a bag lady — alone, poor, old and scared.

Liz

Life isn't fair. I work hard for my money and don't have much to show for it. I just want to quit.

Judy

I just get the rent paid for this month and I have to turn around and start to get the rent money for next month. I never do anything but pay for four crummy walls and a roof. There's never any money for fun. Or if I take some money for fun, I'm late with my rent and my landlord threatens me.

Janet

She can't make as much as I do, and she just bought a new car. My rust bucket is almost nine years old. I don't know what I'm doing wrong.

Denise

I'm just sick and tired of always feeling broke . . . of always being worried.

Suzanne

If I have money, I spend it. I can't help it, there's always something I need.

Jane

I'm making a lot of money. More than I ever dreamed I'd make. But I'm just as scared as when I was a poor student and didn't have any money at all.

Joanne

No matter which way I add up the money, there never is enough.

Mari

Money is always so hard.

Beth

The list of women such as these, speaking about their individual pain and frustration with money, could go on and on and on. Maybe you, too, have felt some of the same painful, frustrating, discouraging, hopeless and scary feelings that these women are expressing. If you have, how would you express your feelings?

Open up your notebook to the first page. It is time to begin recording your personal journey of financial empowerment.

If you have ever had these same painful, frustrating, discouraging, hopeless or scary feelings, how would *you* express these feelings? What words would you use? In your notebook, write down the words you would use to express your feelings about money.

_____

_____

_____

As a result of these painful and frustrating feelings about money, many women decide something must be wrong with them. You may feel that way, too.

You may think, "If only I were more disciplined, maybe I wouldn't be so frustrated." Or, "If only I were a little more attractive, maybe someone else would fix this pain." Or, "If only I were a little better educated . . . or a little more outgoing . . . or a little smarter . . . or a little more lovable . . . or had a little better personality." Or, "If only I were a little better in math . . . *then* maybe I wouldn't be in such trouble with money."

I listen to many, many women ask themselves:

- *"What's the matter with me* that I can't control my spending?"
- *"What's the matter with me* that I just do money so crazy?"
- *"What's the matter with me* that I overdraw my checking account?"
- *"What's the matter with me* that I can't seem to earn more money?"
- *"What's the matter with me* that I have no one to take care of me?"
- *"What's the matter with me* that I so often feel anxious and frustrated about money? I feel like I don't know

what I'm doing. And because I don't know what I'm doing, I'm afraid something bad is going to happen."
- *"What's the matter with me* that I can be in charge of all that money at work, yet if people at work found out how I handle my own money, I'd feel very embarrassed."

Stop reading for a moment and think of all your feelings about you and your money. Do you blame yourself?

Use your notebook to record your feelings about you and your money.

In your notebook, complete the question:

What's the matter with me that I _____

_____

_____

All right, put your pen down and take a good look at yourself.

You are a smart, clever, capable, responsible woman in many other areas of your life. But when it comes to money, sometimes you may feel discouragement and a sense of failure. Sometimes you may feel that it is all very confusing and out of control. Sometimes you may feel incompetent and you may feel shame. Sometimes you may feel that no matter what you do, nothing really works.

What's the problem? Why do you behave the way you do with your money?

If you want to change your behavior — any behavior — you *don't* start with changing that specific behavior. Yet that's what many women try to do.

If you are like many women, you may try to *will* your behavior to change. You may try to get *disciplined* enough to change your behavior. It doesn't work. Just about the time you start to think you are finally getting "good" — then boom, you're down. Something happens. All the good intentions are gone. You're back behaving in the same old way.

The same thing happens if you are trying to change your *money* behavior. Willing yourself to change the way you manage your money doesn't work. Trying to get more disciplined with your money doesn't work either.

Again, just about the time you think you are getting quite "good" with your money, and your budget is finally working . . . then boom, you're down! All your wonderful, responsible, adult money behavior just disappears:

You spend the money you were saving for the next car insurance . . .

- You overdraw your checking account . . .
- You have to call your parents again . . .
- You're at your limit on your credit card . . .
- You get a call from your bank . . .

What happened?

- *"What's the matter with me?"* you ask. "Am I just stupid, or what?"

You aren't stupid. You are smart enough to use the basic skills of personal money management.

So what happened?

---

*If you are frustrated enough to pick up this book, and your sense of frustration is **not** about how smart you are, then . . .*

The problem is with your money training.

"What money training?" you ask.

*Bingo! That's the problem — you have had **no** positive, useful money training.*

There is nothing the matter with you. Your beliefs about money and the way you manage your money — your money behavior — are a reflection of what you've been taught ever since childhood.

As a child, you probably didn't even realize you were being taught about money. You were taught by what you observed and by what you were told by parents, teachers, relatives and friends. You overheard comments by adults. You were taught by images on television and pictures in magazines. What you learned this way, you accepted as truth — whether it was or not.

What you've learned about money — your money training — is only a mirror image that reflects the attitudes, values and beliefs of the people and society that raised you.

Your money training is a mirror that reflects the money attitudes and beliefs of your mother.

Your money training reflects the money attitudes and beliefs of your father, which may not be the same as those of your mother.

Your money training reflects the beliefs and attitudes of the society you live in. This society has taught you much about how you as a woman should behave with money — what you should and should not do, what you can and cannot do.

Since money is what we exchange in this society to get what we want and need, this childhood training affects us deeply.

MONEY

TRAINING

Children learn from their childhood training. As a young girl you were like a little sponge. You soaked in an understanding of how people responded to you when you wanted or needed something. You soaked up all that you heard about how others got what they wanted and needed. You watched and you listened. You may have soaked up fear. You may have soaked up shame. You may have soaked up many feelings about being undeserving and incompetent.

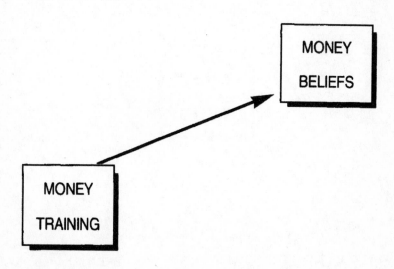

Your childhood money training set your adult attitudes and beliefs about how to get what you want and need. Moreover, your childhood money training set your adult attitudes and beliefs about your *right* to get what you want and need.

This childhood training taught you your personal attitudes and beliefs about money:

- What do I deserve?
- Am I smart enough?
- Do I have to or will someone else do it?
- When do others think I am good?
- When am I lovable?
- When am I acceptable?
- When do I feel safe?

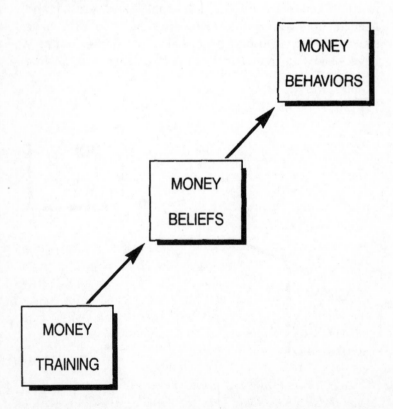

These same money attitudes and beliefs control your adult money behaviors:

- Why do I always spend more than I have?
- Why don't I know the balance in my checkbook?
- Why is it so hard to stay on a budget?
- Why is it so hard for me to sit down and pay my bills?
- Why do I get so angry when I have to pay my bills?
- Why is it so hard to mail my bills?
- Why don't I ever get ahead?

If you want to change your money behaviors, don't begin by trying to change the behaviors themselves. It will never work. Your behaviors will not change. You can't *will* yourself to stop spending. You can't *will* yourself not to be angry when you pay your bills. You can't *will* yourself to get a balance in your checkbook. It'll never work.

If you want to change your money behaviors, you must begin by exploring your childhood money training, by asking yourself, "What did I learn about money and when did I learn it?"

Once you understand what you learned about money, you can then *identify* your specific money beliefs. These money beliefs are your personal, direct response to your childhood money training, and they directly control your adult money behaviors. You will identify these learned money beliefs in chapter 3, "Why Is Money So Hard For Me?" And you will identify your adult money behaviors in chapter 4, "No Matter What I Do, It Doesn't Work."

You *can* change your money life. In Part II, "Unlearning the Learning," you will begin to understand that when you allow yourself to clearly identify both your learned money beliefs and the resulting money behaviors, you can then *un*learn these money beliefs. *Un*learning your learned money beliefs makes it possible for you to decide to change your adult money behaviors.

Your money beliefs and your money behaviors are a result of your childhood training. They are not a result of some inherent problem or defect in you. If you can begin to reach this level of acceptance, then you will be able to begin the process of changing your money beliefs and your money behaviors. You'll begin by asking yourself, "How did I get this way?"

৯ TWO ৯

How Did I Get This Way?

The way you act with your money — your money be-haviors — is a direct result of your money beliefs. The way you think about money — your money beliefs — was learned in your childhood. So you act the way you do with your money because of your childhood learning.

If you will allow yourself to see your childhood training clearly, you will begin to understand why you have been so stuck and frustrated with your money. Understanding your childhood money training is the first step in making a change in your money life.

In this chapter you will spend some time exploring your childhood money training by answering questions in a personal money inventory. Your responses will answer the question, "What did I learn?"

These questions came out of the "Women and Money" classes that I teach. When we do the inventory in class, I tell the women that it's all right for them to copy from each other. We need to help each other as women to remember our childhood money training. We need to help each other remember that the statement, "This is just the way I am and always have been" needs to be changed to, "This is the way I was trained, and I can change my training."

To give you the same opportunity to get help from other women in identifying your training and unlocking your childhood memories, I have included responses that women in my classes have made to some of the inventory questions. If their responses get in your way of remembering, please ignore them. If they help, I'm glad.

For example, Kathryn, a 36-year-old computer analyst, told the class, "I was raised in an alcoholic family. I have spent years in therapy and 12-Step groups dealing with issues concerning the emotionally unhealthy training I had in this family system. In all these years, it never entered my mind that the way I thought about money and how I actually managed my money had any relationship at all to that family system. I just thought I was bad with money because I couldn't make myself be disciplined enough. Now I understand it isn't just a matter of discipline. It's not a matter of me being bad. In the same way I looked at my drinking, I need to look at what my family taught me when I was a child that isn't healthy for me now. Only this time, I'm looking at my money."

Please have your notebook ready to record your personal journey of financial empowerment. Record your responses to the inventory questions in this notebook. Please be patient with yourself and take your time as you work through this inventory.

Settle down with your notebook and pen. Allow yourself to go back in time to when you were a very young girl. Allow yourself to feel the feelings you felt as this young, dependent, innocent little girl.

Personal Money Inventory

1. What age are you? Where do you live? With whom?

2. How much money did your family have? Were you really poor? Not poor, but not rich? Sort of rich? Rich? How did you know this as a very young girl?

3. Did you have about the same amount of money as your friends? Less? More? How did you know?

I've always felt different because my dad was a doctor and we always had more money. I've always felt like I had to do more, buy more, pick up the tab more in order for me to have friends. You know, I still feel like I have to do more, and most of my friends have more money than I do. I wonder if I think I have to buy friendships.

Pam

We were always poor. I can remember not going to school because I didn't have clothes to wear. We got what was left over from the relatives. I always felt shabby. Even now, I can spend money on a very nice outfit and it still looks poor to me. I feel like I still don't fit in.

Janet

4. What does it mean to belong? As a child did you feel like you belonged anywhere? Family? Friends? Church?

5. When you really *needed* something, like gym shoes for school or a notebook, which adult did you ask? What happened when you asked?

6. When you really *wanted* something that was pretty or fun, which adult did you ask? What happened when you asked?

I learned not to ask because when I asked, whether it was a 25-cent notebook or a pair of shoes, it was treated as the opening of World War III. It wasn't worth it ever to ask. When I was older, I started babysitting as soon as I could. Then I didn't ever have to ask for money again.

Anne

This sounds terrible, but I'd wait to catch Dad in a good mood. If I waited, I could get anything I wanted, especially if he was feeling guilty about his drinking.

Kathryn

I don't ever remember asking for anything because somehow my mother always guessed what I wanted. I really hated some of the stuff she bought me. I didn't want to wear some of it, but I figured it wasn't worth the hassle. And having stuff I didn't like was still better than making her mad and not having any stuff.

Judy

7. Whose job was it to *earn* the money for your family?

8. Whose job was it to *spend* the money for your family? As a little girl, who did you believe had the real control and power with the money? Try to remember scenes from your childhood that gave you this belief.

My mom did the bills and bought us things. But I remember her asking my dad if she could do this or that. He always had the final say.

Denise

My mom didn't trust my dad with money. He was paid every Friday, and he had to come directly home from work after he cashed his paycheck and give it to her. If he needed gas for the car, he had to ask her. She always seemed scared on Fridays until he came home.

Beth

If I needed a notebook, I went to my mother. If I needed something big, I went to my father.

Jane

9. As you got older, do you remember people talking about money in your family or was it a taboo subject? If money was talked about, what did you hear? Try to remember what people said.

My mom was always angry about money and she was always angry at my father. If only he was a little smarter or worked a little harder or had done anything more than what he was doing, then maybe we wouldn't always be so broke.

Joanne

I remember my dad hollering at my mother. He would accuse her of being totally irresponsible about money because she spent too much money on us kids. I would hear

her try to explain but he would holler louder. Then I remember her crying.

Mari

I can't remember anyone ever talking about money. I don't
think I even knew we had bills. We lived in a small town,
and when I would go to the grocery store to get some stuff
for home, they just wrote it down. I don't even remember
realizing that someone would have to pay for it.

Pat

I remember my mother crying and saying, "Nothing ever
changes. No matter what I do, there is never enough." I
remember her tired all the time.

Suzanne

10. Did you feel that you had power or control as a
    member of your family? Did you have any say, or
    were you ever asked what you thought about pur-
    chases that were made, where you moved, what
    kind of home your family lived in or if there was to
    be a job change for one of your parents?

11. As a young girl, did you ever have money of your
    own? At what age? Was it an allowance? Earned
    money? What memories do you have about the
    adults' reactions to how you spent your money?

In grade school I remember getting a quarter each week. I
realized I could get one 5-cent cone each day after school. I
was proud of myself because I didn't buy gum or a comic
book or anything. Each day I took my nickel to the store and
bought my cone. One night, at dinner, my father told the
rest of my family what I did with my quarter. It was a joke
and they were laughing at me because I was silly. I felt
confused and hurt. I had thought I was so clever with my
money. I stopped buying my cones. I don't remember what
I spent my money on after that.

Jennifer

I started babysitting when I was 12. I saved half of all the
money I earned for a red bike. When I had saved almost
enough, I told my mother what I was going to get. She told
me I was selfish because our family needed the money more

than I needed a bike. I gave her the money. I don't remember ever saving for anything again. What's the point?

Vickie

Our family has always had more money than my friends' families. I never got an allowance, but I got everything I asked for. The lady next door asked if I would walk her dog and she would pay me 10 cents a day. I had seen this doll I liked at the store and I decided to put my dimes in my dresser until I had enough for the doll. I saved and saved until there were a lot of dimes. My mother found the dimes one day. She asked what the dimes were for and I told her. The next day I came home from school and on my bed were two dolls. They were twins of the doll I wanted. My dad told me he thought it was cute of me to try to save, but it wasn't necessary and that he would get me what I wanted.

Denise

12. **What did you hear from your family about people who had money? Were poor women "better" than rich women? Or was it better to be rich than poor?**

In junior high I had two special friends. The father of one of my friends had died, and her mother had four kids. They didn't have much money. My mother always called my friend's mother a "saint." My other friend's father was a bank vice-president. My mother didn't like her mother and used to call her a "rich bitch."

Mari

My mom always said, "Marry a doctor. Don't be poor like us." When I was in college, I brought home a guy I was dating who was a pre-med student and came from lots of money. I wanted our two families to have dinner together, but my mom refused. She said they weren't 'our kind of people.'

Jean

My father always said that it was the rich people's fault that we had wars and poor people. He said it was their fault for everything bad. He said that even though we didn't have much, at least people liked us and knew we weren't bad.

Liz

13. As a young girl, when do you remember getting approval? When were you complimented? When did you feel loved?

When I was good.

Beth

When I looked cute.

Kay

When I was polite and nice.

Judy

14. What did you learn about the need to take care of yourself?

Everyone told me I was "cute as a button" when I was a little girl. My dad told me someday some handsome rich man would come and 'sweep me off my feet' and take care of me. All I had to do was to stay cute and sweet.

Kay

All of us girls spent most of our babysitting money on makeup and hair and stuff. My job, as I understood it, was to look good enough and be nice enough without being too smart so some man would fall in love with me and take care of me.

Judy

My mother would say to me, "Don't ever do what I did and trust a man like I did or you'll end up like me. You'll be stuck without a decent education and with a bunch of kids." And I remember not believing her. I remember thinking there must be something wrong with her because my dad didn't take care of her better. I remember day-dreaming that it would be different for me because I'd be loved and taken care of.

Suzanne

I remember being told at home and in church that God would provide. As long as I did what God taught and was a good and loving girl and became a good and loving woman, God would love me and take care of me.

Beth

15. What does it mean to be safe? Did you ever feel safe as a young girl? When? If you didn't feel safe as a young girl, what was happening in your family home so you didn't feel safe?

In some ways we were safe. We always had plenty of food. But safe? I don't know. That's really hard. I always felt invisible in my home. I never got what I wanted for gifts. My parents were always so busy with the store. I always have this ache inside. Safe? I don't know.

Joanne

Huh? I don't know what you mean by safe.

Jane

No! No! Never safe! I had plenty of clothes, allowance, food and even a car when I was a teenager. All my friends thought I was so lucky. But the price was high. My father sexually abused me for almost four years. I was always scared. I knew as a child I couldn't protect and take care of myself. I still don't seem to be able to do that.

Anne

I never knew what was going to happen next. I didn't know if my dad would come home. I didn't know if we would move again. I didn't know if there would be food. I didn't know if I would get the notebook for school. I didn't know if I would get hit or my sister or my mother would get hit. I was always waiting to see if I would be all right. I was always scared inside. And there was no one to talk to.

Kathryn

16. Are there any other questions *you* want to ask *yourself* to make your money training complete? What other remembering do you need to do so that the picture of your childhood money training is absolutely clear to you?

You've done a lot of remembering: some painful, some pleasurable, but all of it informative.

Look at the responses you wrote in your notebook. Relax for a minute and take a deep breath as you form a picture in your mind of that young, dependent, innocent little girl you used to be. Picture this little girl — *you* — as a soft sponge who absorbed all these childhood experiences. As this little girl, you absorbed and you learned. You learned who made the choices with money — who had money power. You learned how to get what you needed — maybe. You learned how to get what you wanted — maybe. You learned what you were supposed to do to get what you wanted, what someone else had to do. You learned what you deserved — or didn't deserve. You learned what it meant to be safe — maybe.

Close your eyes for just a minute and feel the feelings of that little girl. Feel all her experiences — all her training.

In your notebook write down a few words or a few sentences to explain what you have just felt as you pictured this little girl — *you*. Writing will help you remember this impressionable, dependent little girl so that you never forget that how you think about getting what you want and need (your money beliefs) and how you act with your money (your money behaviors) all come back to this little girl — *you* — and her childhood money training.

◈ THREE ◈

WHY IS MONEY SO HARD FOR ME?

If money is hard for you, it is because your learned money beliefs keep tripping you up. These learned money beliefs are simply your emotional responses to your childhood money training. They stop you from adopting new, more positive ways to manage your money. The ways you work with and manage your money are called your *money behaviors*.

Your process of continually *willing* your money behavior to change may feel like trying continually, painstakingly and unsuccessfully to climb a huge emotional boulder. This emotional boulder is your own personal belief barrier to changing your money behaviors. It consists of all the words you learned to say to yourself — as a little girl — in response to your childhood money training. Whenever you try to make changes in your adult money behavior — how you work with and how you manage your money — you are confronted by this overwhelming emotional boulder.

The money beliefs that make up your emotional boulder are neither good nor bad. They are simply your emotional response to your childhood money training. Some of your money beliefs are useful in your adult life and some are not. Some of your learned emotional responses work and some create unworkable money behaviors. Some of your beliefs have hurt you and some have not.

However, *if* the ways you have been working with and managing your money are not working, and *if* you felt frustrated and discouraged when you tried to change your money behaviors, *then* you know for sure that at least some of your money beliefs are not useful to your adult money life. You have learned some unworkable money beliefs as part of your emotional responses to your childhood money training.

If you are tired of feeling frustrated by how difficult dealing with money is for you, then you will want to spend some time identifying the specific money beliefs that are not useful to you as an adult. What are the specific money beliefs that have stopped you from changing your unworkable and hurtful money behavior? What are the specific money beliefs that make up this huge emotional boulder that stops you from changing your unworkable and hurtful money behavior?

Do you see that your personal money belief boulder is separate from you? Your money beliefs are external to the real you. These learned money beliefs, which are the words you say to yourself, are not really you. They are *not* an innate part of you. They are *not* a defect in you. These money beliefs are simply words that you learned to say to yourself in your childhood money training, and now they are creating an emotional barrier to change in your money behaviors.

At this point you, like many women in my classes, may be saying, "I don't know what you mean by money beliefs." To find out, take this True/False exercise.

True Or False

Directions: Mark "T" if the statement is something you say or have said to yourself. Mark "F" if you have never made the statement to yourself.

_____ I've never been any good with numbers.

_____ I shouldn't have to manage the money, someone else will.

_____ There's never enough money, no matter what.

_____ Them that has, gets.

_____ Checking accounts are confusing.

_____ If I get good at money, it'll be harder to find someone to love me.

_____ I trust The Universe to take care of me.

_____ I can't _____

_____ I don't want to be one of "them."

_____ I don't have the discipline to be good with money.

_____ I'm not smart enough.

_____ If I'm truly lovable and good and if I care for others more than myself, someone else will take care of me.

_____ I'm not left-brained enough to do money.

_____ I don't want to, so I shouldn't have to.

_____ God will provide.

_____ I could never handle money.

_____ It will all work out. It always has and always will.

_____ There's never enough.

_____ Women take care of the relationships. Men take care of the money.

_____ Good women will be taken care of.

_____ I'm compulsive with money.

_____ If I earn a lot of money, people at work will expect more of me than I can do.

_____ If I earn a lot of money, I will always have to be saying "no" to people. I'm not good at saying "no."

_____ Information about money is in the hands of only a few people — mostly men.

_____ I can always find someone to take care of me.

_____ Men don't like women who know as much or more about money than they do.

_____ Women are the emotional caretakers. Men are the wage earners.

_____ Prosperity is just a state of mind.

_____ Money means power and power means abuse.

_____ I always ask for too much.

_____ I should be more comfortable with less.

Are there any other statements that are true for you that you'd like to add to this list?

T _____

T _____

T _____

T _____

T _____

All the statements you marked "T" are your learned money beliefs. These money beliefs are your learned emotional responses, which come straight from your childhood money training.

If you don't believe me, check it out. Take a few minutes and look back in your notebook and check out your responses to the personal money inventory you took in the last chapter.

Do you see the connection between your childhood money training and your adult money beliefs? Can you identify the specific childhood training that taught you these adult money beliefs?

These responses from other women may help you identify this connection:

My training: I remember when I was in ninth grade and I was going to sign up for algebra. My school counselor told me he didn't think I was smart enough for algebra and I should take business math instead, because anyone could pass that class. He told me I was such a cutie that I would never need algebra anyway, so why worry my pretty little head.

My adult money belief: I'm not smart enough. I won't need to be smart because I'm cute.

Pam

My training: My mom told me, "You've taken all the money you've ever had and just blown it."

My adult money belief: I could never handle money right.

Joanne

My training: I remember being hollered at for always wasting money. I was told that money just ran through my fingers like water. I was told I was completely undisciplined, and that giving money to me was the same as flushing the money down the toilet.

My adult money belief: I'm a compulsive overspender. I can't trust myself. I have no discipline.

Sara

My training: I remember my math teacher joking that the only reason I passed his class was because I did all the extra-credit work.

My adult money belief: I'm no good with numbers.

Beth

My training: I got so confused because when I was a kid my mother told me that if I ever wanted anything, I'd need to get it myself. I could never trust a man. Yet somehow I learned that if I was nice enough and looked good, I could get a husband who would love me and take care of me and I wouldn't have to worry. It's as if one message was spoken, but the other message was there, too.

My adult money belief: Confusion! I feel like my life is on hold. I don't know what to believe so what I believe is that if I just wait patiently, I'll find out which way I can be safe. I just wait.

Pat

My training: I can remember my grandmother, my mother and my Aunt Nicky all telling me how lucky I was that I was pretty because then I would always have someone to take care of me.

My adult money belief: I shouldn't have to worry about money. Someone else will do that.

Mari

My training: When I was about seven years old, I remember telling my mother I wanted to be an astronaut. She gave me a hug and said, "Why don't you become a mommy? You have to be real smart to become an astronaut. Wouldn't you rather get married and have children, like me?"

My adult money belief: I'm not smart enough to be anything but married.

Judy

The childhood money training these women experienced really did result in very specific beliefs about them and their money. Now you can begin to see the connection between your own childhood money training and your own adult money beliefs.

Open up your notebook again. Write down your specific childhood money training and the resulting adult money belief that was the result of this specific childhood training. Use this form:

My money training was _____

_____

My resulting adult money belief is _____

_____

Identify as many of these connections between your childhood money training and adult money beliefs as you can remember right now.

You may feel embarrassed to admit that you really believe some of these adult money beliefs. Some of these beliefs may seem irrational. Some may seem silly. Some simplistic. Some maddening. Some scary. But it's important to be truthful. Why? Because all of these beliefs are *your* beliefs, and *your* beliefs have had a profound influence on stopping you from changing the way you work with and manage your money. *Your* beliefs have had a profound capability to stop you from changing your unworkable and hurtful money behaviors.

Remember, beliefs are an *emotional* response to an experience. Money beliefs are an *emotional* response to childhood learned money experiences. Sometimes emotional responses really are irrational — they don't make sense in the intellectual world. Sometimes they are simplistic, maddening or scary. Emotional responses are emotional — that's what they are. Emotional responses — beliefs — come from a feeling response to some experience. Just because a belief comes from an emotional feeling rather than an intellectual or rational response, however, doesn't make the belief any less real.

All beliefs are real, and beliefs always affect behavior. *Always.* If I say to my partner, "I love you," that statement is an emotional response to an experience. Even though that emotional response may be irrational, it is very real and will directly affect my behavior toward my partner. If I see a tornado coming my way, I may say, "I'm scared" as an emotional response to the swirling cloud. That emotional response will directly affect my behavior — I will run for shelter.

Money beliefs are a learned emotional response to an experience. That's why money beliefs don't always make sense. But just because money beliefs are *feeling* based and not intellectually based doesn't make them any less real. Your money beliefs absolutely and directly affect your money behavior — whether you want them to or not.

Your learned money beliefs have enormous power and control over your money behavior. They have this power and control *whether or not they make sense; whether or not they are true.* Many, maybe even most of your money beliefs are simply *not* true in light of your real life experiences. What you've learned to believe about you and your money does not fit with what you've experienced in your money life. Here you've been believing all these years, and these money beliefs simply aren't true. You've learned to believe one thing, and your life experiences with money are something entirely different. Because of this you may feel hurt, angry, confused and maybe even betrayed. You keep on asking yourself: "Why is it that what I believe is *supposed* to happen in my money life never seems to fit with what *really* happens in my money life?"

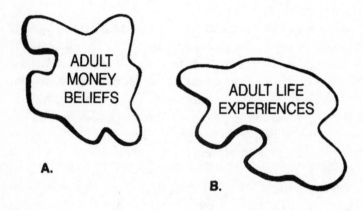

This person which is you —
— this wonderful
　scared
　　caring
　　　frustrated
　　　loving
　　　　rebellious
　　　　hopeful
　　　　　defiant
　　　　　patient
　　　　　　deprived
　　　　　strong
　　　　　　vulnerable
　　　　　　prosperous
　　　　　　tired
　　　　　　confused
　　　　　　　smart woman —
— is like a giant puzzle made up of many puzzle pieces.

You have been trying for years to find a way to make these money belief puzzle pieces fit together with your life experience puzzle pieces. You believe that if you can get all these puzzle pieces — your adult money beliefs and your actual life experiences — to fit together, then maybe life and money wouldn't be so hard. You believe you would know what to do with your money and be able to do it. You believe the puzzle pieces would fit together easily. You believe if you could get your money belief puzzle pieces and your money behavior puzzle pieces to fit, your money life would work.

You're right. If all of your puzzle pieces — your beliefs and your life experiences — really did fit together, you would never have picked up this book. You wouldn't have needed it because your money life would be fine. You would work with and manage your money easily and clearly. You would have no emotional boulder in your money life that you keep trying to climb. You would have no inner conflict.

Without this inner conflict, your money life would be fine because you would be capable of learning personal money management skills. Without this inner conflict, all you would need is your own smarts and a five-dollar calculator. Do you remember when you decided this?

But if you have a conflict within you between what you believe should happen in your money life and what *really does* happen in your money life . . .

And if you have no way to resolve that conflict other than to criticize yourself and wonder, "Where did I mess up again? What's the matter with me?". . .

Then money is hard. Money is confusing. Money and decisions about money all feel so crazy. You feel bad about yourself. You hurt. You are confused and scared because your basic personal beliefs are in conflict with your real-life experiences. Your money and your life feel unmanageable and out of control.

Instead of challenging your learned personal beliefs, however, you — like many other women — may start to criticize yourself. In order to resolve this inner emotional conflict, you may tell yourself, "There must be something wrong with me." You may tell yourself that you are wrong rather than deciding your beliefs are wrong and need to be changed.

> I always feel bad about myself. It's as if I'm never good enough. My life seems like such a struggle. Every time I meet a nice guy, I think, "Maybe this will be the one who'll take care of all my money problems and then everything will be different." I'm kind of embarrassed to even admit it, but it's true. So I try to look nice and be fun and think that if it works, "someone else can do the worrying instead of me."
>
> *Vickie*
>
> I just never think about money. I suppose I'll have to eventually, or I'll be a bag lady. Boy, that's scary. But I keep thinking maybe something will happen — maybe I'll meet someone or win the Publisher's Clearing House Sweepstakes . . .
>
> *Joanne*

Do you hear the conflict? "I know I should be doing something different because this isn't working. But . . .."

Picking up this book means that you are experiencing a conflict between what you believe to be true about you and your money, and what you have actually experienced in your life. Because of this inner conflict, your personal puzzle pieces may look like this:

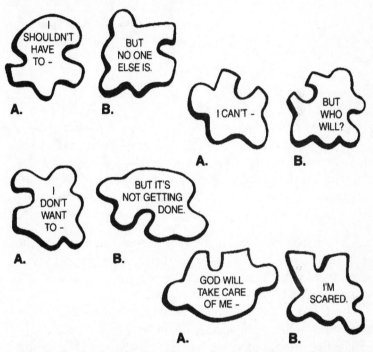

If you look closely, you'll see that each learned money belief puzzle piece doesn't fit with each life experience puzzle piece.

It's time to be honest about the conflict between your childhood learned money beliefs and what you are actually experiencing in your money life. It's time to record this conflict in your notebook.

The following are four pairs of puzzle pieces that do *not* fit together. In each pair, write your learned money belief in one piece and your adult life experience in the other piece.

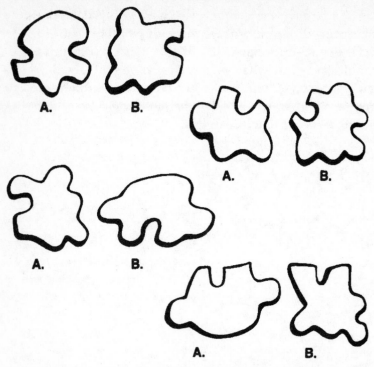

It's time to tell yourself the truth. Your life experiences with money are real. That is the truth. Your experiences with money have been difficult, frustrating and a bit scary. That is the truth. That is real.

The truth is you have an unworkable problem in your money life when each money belief is paired with a difficult, frustrating and scary money experience. The truth is that something isn't working. If you have decided that you can't *will* your money behavior to change because *willing* behavior to change doesn't work, then you will want to look to your money beliefs for change. You learned these beliefs as part of an emotional response to a childhood experience. These money beliefs are supposed to keep you safe and happy in your adult life experiences. The truth is that these learned money beliefs do not and have not kept you safe and happy. The truth is that you will need to change these learned money beliefs if you want to be financially safe and happy.

For much of your life you have wondered, "What's the matter with me that money is so hard? That money is such a problem for me?"

Remember, the truth is that nothing is the matter with you. Money is hard and a problem for you because your learned money beliefs are keeping you from learning new, workable and empowering money behaviors. The truth is that you will want to change these learned money beliefs so that you can change your money behaviors.

ॐ FOUR ॐ

No Matter What I Do, It Doesn't Work.

In this society many women are taught:

- We don't want to manage money — so we don't.
- We shouldn't have to — so we don't.
- Money is too hard — so we don't do it.

Many women are also taught to believe that *if*:

- We are loving enough
- We are caring enough
- We are pretty enough
- We are nurturing enough

Then we will be taken care of financially. We will be provided for. A man, God, the Universe — somebody or something *outside of ourselves* will take care of us. Somehow, some way, everything will work out. We will be all right. We will finally be financially safe.

These money beliefs, which are based on childhood money training, have not worked for most women. These beliefs have not created safety for women. Women are not financially safe. These beliefs are a lie.

The consequences of living a life based on a belief system of lies have been emotionally and financially disastrous for many, many women in this society.

In the last chapter you identified the emotional trauma of living a life based on false money beliefs. You identified the emotional exhaustion of trying to climb your personal money belief boulder. You identified the emotional confusion of trying to understand "What's the matter with me?" as you keep trying to resolve the conflict between what you learned to be true — your money beliefs — and what you actually experience in your adult money life — your money behavior. You began to understand the *emotional consequences* of basing your life on learned money beliefs that are not true and that do not work.

The *consequences* of living a life based on money beliefs that aren't true and don't work go well beyond emotional consequences. The *financial consequences* in women's lives have been devastating:

- Right now, the poverty class in this country is almost entirely women and their children. Even with all the increased awareness of women, the financial statistics don't appear to be getting measurably better. The predictions are that by the early 21st century, women alone and women with children, will make up almost the entire poverty class.
- There are more than 51 million women in this country. Of that 51 million, it is estimated that only 2 million earn $25,000 or more.
- Half the women working today have no pension plan.
- The median income for older women is barely above poverty level. Right now, about 80 percent of all retired women have no pension plan. When women get old, they end up alone, poor and scared.

Liz, a woman in one of my "Women and Money" classes, put it this way:

"I read," said Liz, "that 90 percent of the female population is earning less than $25,000 a year. I also read that most of us women aren't even concerned about being old and poor. That's crazy!"

She stood up and hit her fist against her open palm. "No wonder we're seen as naive about money. Anyone with any smarts should be scared by statistics like these. I'm scared. What do we think is going to happen? Who do we think is going to fix this? The divorce rate is about 50 percent. Men die before women, and the Social Security system looks like it's running out of money."

Liz sat down and continued in a soft voice, "I'm 54 years old. I've been in a responsible management position for almost eight years. I'm supposed to retire from my job in 11 years, and all I have is a company retirement. I have no savings. All these years I've just paid my bills and lived from paycheck to paycheck. I have no back-up. I think I make more money than many women and I'm still scared."

It's frightening to:

- not know if you can pay your bills.
- feel powerless and scared.
- feel uneasy with money decisions.
- worry about being a bag lady.
- have people call and harass you for money.
- not have anyone who will take care of the money.
- not have any savings.
- wait and wonder, "What's the matter with me?"

In your notebook, complete this sentence:
What frightens me most about me and my money life is

_____

_____

_____ .

What else frightens me? _____

_____

_____ .

As a woman, the financial consequences of this unre-solved conflict between your learned money beliefs and what really happens in your life experiences can be truly frightening. The financial consequences of not knowing what to do to be financially safe, as a woman, can be truly frightening.

Let's stop for a minute. How are you doing? In my "Women and Money" classes, talking about this fear is one of the most difficult places for the women to get through. It's a scary place. It's scary to look at the financial consequences of this unresolved conflict. It's scary because it's difficult to see any solutions to this problem of money.

Where you are right now in this book may feel to you like being in the middle of a nightmare. It is the nightmare of no solution to the problem.

Your nightmare may be about a terrifying monster in your bedroom closet. You wake up from the nightmare and lie there, trying to decide if there really *is* a life-threatening monster in your closet. You squint your eyes and try to see the closet door through the darkness. "Is the closet door still closed?" you ask yourself. Maybe the door is moving and the monster is coming out to get you. You're frightened. You pull the covers over your head, pretending you are safe. But there still may be a monster in your closet. You realize that your bed covers will not protect you from the monster. You feel even more frightened.

When you can't stand the suspense any longer, you take a deep breath and slide out of bed. You walk softly toward the closed door. Then you do the most frightening thing you can do: One hand flips on the light switch, while the other hand yanks open the closet door.

Fear! Terror! Even though you are scared, you look directly at your monster. How big is your monster? Will your monster hurt you? How life-threatening is this monster of yours? The scariest place to be right now is standing in front of the open closet door looking at your monster.

You are in the most fear-producing place in this book, *right now.* You are looking at your financial monster — the financial consequences of your learned money beliefs. You have the light on and the door open. You're telling yourself the truth.

You're all right. The monster will not get you. Honest identification of this monster — your financial consequences — is the only truly safe step you can take right now. Once you have honestly identified your monster, then you can learn ways to protect yourself. You can learn ways to live your life without this monster. Section II, "Unlearning The Learning," will help you learn new and safer ways to live.

Right now, however, you have the light on and are looking at your monster. You are still in the process of honestly identifying the financial consequences of this unresolved conflict between your learned beliefs and your adult life experiences.

This is the place in my classes where I ask the women to honestly identify their financial monsters to the class. They ask themselves the question: "What is the scariest financial consequence — my monster — that I am facing right now?"

I encourage the women to tell the truth and remind them that they don't have to feel shame, embarrassment, stupidity and all t' ∗ other judgments with which women are so quick to 1   themselves. They tell themselves, just like you wi¹   ant to tell yourself, that this is not about who they   ε as people. They are intelligent, competent, caring, ⸀ owing, recovering women.

You can enjoy the same benefit the women in the class have. Without shame or judgment, they listen to other women speak of the financial consequences in their lives. In the class there is always an initial sense of fear, and then a sense of relief and letting go. Because as each woman listens to the other capable, smart, caring, growing women, she begins to really *know* for herself that these financial consequences are a result of her money training, not a reflection of who she is as a person.

> But what am I going to do? I'm 67 years old, and all I have
> is my husband's Social Security. I'm frightened. Instead of

feeling sadness because he died, all I feel is anger. I feel betrayed. He told me I would be all right. And I'm not. What am I going to do?

Suzanne

I keep getting these overdraft notices. At least they look like overdraft notices. I don't know for sure because I haven't opened them because I don't know what to do about it anyway. Now people are calling about their returned checks. Today the bank called and said my checking account would be closed as of today. I don't know what to do. I don't even know where to start.

Denise

I'm a nurse. I was going to get a four-year nursing degree, but I know how hard math is for me so I decided I'd never make it. I never even tried, and now I'm stuck in a nursing job that's low-paying and has rotating shifts. I'm not much more than a nursing assistant. I'm broke and discouraged.

Joanne

I just get by. My two brothers both own homes, and one of them has his own company. I rent a one-bedroom apartment. My car is eight years old and keeps breaking down. My dad gave me money for the last repair. I hate my job. I start to look for another one and then just give up.

Mari

Do you notice any similarities between your financial consequences and the financial consequences of these women?

Manage my money? I don't even think about money. I keep a telephone answering machine on all the time so I can screen calls. That's how I avoid the bill collectors. I pay my phone and my rent. That's all I do.

Beth

He just left. Can you believe that? He just left me here with the kids. I have no money, so I applied for assistance today. Even if I could find a job, who would take care of the kids? I did everything I was supposed to do. I made babies, cooked good meals, went to bed with him. And he abandoned me. I feel stupid because I believed him and I'm scared.

Pam

It's just always hard. We save some money. Then we need a repair on the house or something. We just never get ahead. I'm tired and it's hard.

Kathryn

I owe $12,426 in back taxes. The IRS is threatening my paychecks and my house. How did this happen? I don't know what to do.

Nickie

How did I get old so fast? I always thought I'd have plenty of time to get my retirement planned. I always thought I'd be planning my retirement with a partner. My partner left me and there was never any extra money to put away. I always thought I'd do it someday. I guess someday never came. I'm trying hard not to panic.

Janet

Now it's your turn. In your notebook, honestly describe the monster you are looking at right now — the financial consequences in your life. Take your time as you look your financial monster in the face.

Now reread what you just wrote. You may be feeling a little sad. Maybe you are feeling some fear. Please remember: You no longer need to live with sadness and fear. You no longer need to live with this financial monster in your life.

You, like the other women who have just described their financial monsters, may finally be understanding that your financial monster really was created by the money training you had as a child, and your resulting money beliefs.

- You may also be realizing that *you learned*, either by words or by actions, that you didn't need to have the skills to manage money — someone else would do that.

See how the financial monster is being created with this learned belief?

- You may be realizing that *you learned* you didn't need to know how and when to pay bills or even if you have to pay them, somehow it would get done and be all right.

And the financial monster gets bigger.

- You may be realizing that *you learned* you didn't need to understand the rules of the credit system and the banks — those rules are for others to understand.

The financial monster keeps growing.

- Or *you learned* that you didn't need to learn how to save for and buy a home — someone else will take charge of saving for and buying a home.
- Or *you learned* that you didn't need to know how to pay estimated taxes — you'll think about that some other time.
- Or *you learned* that you didn't need to save for old age — someone will take care of you.

See how huge your financial monster is now.

None of these childhood learned beliefs are true. You, like many other women, are realizing the enormous, devastating effect these untrue learned beliefs have had on your life. You are realizing how these beliefs have created your financial monster.

You are beginning to realize the fear this financial monster has created in your life:

- the powerlessness
- the confusion
- the chaos
- the shame
- the personal sense of loss.

PART II

UNLEARNING
THE LEARNING

———————

A tall, erect, white-haired, immaculately groomed woman sat across from me at my desk.

"Ruth," she said, "I am 72 years old. I've always had a very gracious life. My husband died of a heart attack when I was 48 years old. He left a considerable estate, or so they told me. I then proceeded to raise our six children to adulthood. I continued my role as homemaker and continued to pay for their school tuition out of the money my husband left."

She paused for breath and then continued, her voice starting to quaver. "He always told me there would be enough money if anything happened to him. I never thought to question this — even after he died."

This time her voice broke, and it took her a while to continue. "I'm out of money. It's gone. I always thought I'd go back to school or travel. But there was always something or someone to take care of, and he did say there would be enough money. Not only have I lost my pride and my dignity, but I'm also completely terrified. I don't know what to do. Who will take care of me now when I can't?" As she finished speaking, she bowed her head and sobbed.

This woman's story had a most profound effect on me in my early years as a financial consultant. This experience also had a most profound effect on me as a woman who had the same societal money training as this woman — the same childhood money training *you* have had.

I had two powerful responses to her story: My heart broke for this proud, terrified woman. I felt overwhelmingly sad for her. *Then* I felt my anger: my anger as a woman and as a teacher. My anger at the emotional and financial consequences of the unresolved conflict between what women are taught to believe will keep them financially safe in this world and the incredible lack of financial safety women actually experience in this world. My anger as a woman and my anger as a professional said, "No more!"

It was out of this heartbreak and anger that I began the "Women and Money" classes. It was out of this heartbreak and anger that I wrote this book.

I want you to meet this woman, because I'm hoping you, too, will feel a sadness and an anger for her. A sadness and an anger for other women and most of all for yourself. A sadness at the pain you have felt as you try and try to make your learned money beliefs keep you financially safe as an adult. An anger and a determination as you say, "No more!"

The second section of this book will help you with your determination to *un*learn the old training that hasn't worked for you as you learn new training that will work to truly keep you financially safe.

❧ FIVE ❧

No More!

All change starts with a decision to change. When you tell yourself, *"No More!"* you are making a decision to change.

When a woman makes a decision to change her money beliefs and her money behaviors, she may say:

- *No More* will I passively accept the money training I had as a child — this training that hasn't worked and isn't working in my life.
- *No More* am I willing to live with the painful conflict between what I was taught about money and what I have actually experienced.
- *No More* am I willing to live with shame.
- *No More* will I live with fear.
- *No More* will I feel left out of taking charge of my life because I don't know the rules about money.
- *No More* am I willing to feel like a victim — helpless and hopeless.

If you want to change your money life, this change also starts with a decision by you to change.

Open the notebook that you are using for your personal journey of financial empowerment and complete this sentence:

No more _____

_____.

How about another one?

No more _____

_____.

Another?

No more _____

_____.

Continue to complete this sentence until you *know* you have made an absolute, unchangeable, resolute commitment to change every area of your money life.

When you are finished, read aloud to yourself the decision sentences you just wrote. Read them *out loud* so your ears really hear your absolute, unchangeable, resolute commitment to change every area of your money life. Do you have any more to add?

Keep reading your sentences out loud until you can *feel* the vibration of this change decision way down to the tips of your toes. If that sounds ridiculous, read the sentences out loud again. Read them until you not only *know* you have made a decision to change, but you can actually *feel* in your body this decision to change.

If you don't actually *feel* this change decision yet, try this: Take your notebook with you and get up out of your chair. Walk around the room and read your change decisions to yourself — out loud. If you're feeling self-conscious, close the door so that you have complete privacy.

It is critical for every part of you to literally *feel* that you have made a decision to change. There are difficult times ahead as you work to make changes in your money life. These difficult times won't seem as difficult if you really and truly can *feel* the decision you have made to change.

I learned this from one of my "Women and Money" classes. The women in this particular class seemed to be highly motivated to make changes in their money lives, but they just weren't making many changes. These women, as an entire class, seemed stuck in their old, frustrating, hopeless money training. They just didn't seem to be able to make any firm money belief changes or money behavior changes.

One day in class, I asked them to get up out of their chairs and move. They all stared at me. I again asked them if they would take their notebooks, get up and move. I asked them to walk around the building reading their change decisions out loud to themselves. With a great deal of self-consciousness, some of the women got up and started reading quietly. Again I encouraged all of them to get up and walk around and begin reading their change decisions out loud to themselves until they could actually *feel* those decisions in their toes.

Soon, all of them began walking around different parts of the building as they read out loud to themselves from their notebooks.

Some minutes later, Joanne, a woman in her late fifties, who had been quite reserved in the class, came walking by me with her fist in the air saying loudly, "No more will I always be so scared about money. I get to decide. I decide not to be scared." And she gave me a big grin as she walked past.

I heard Judy and Beth reading their change decisions to each other. I also heard their delighted laughter.

I saw Pat reading, walking and wiping some tears.

When I attempted to reassemble the class a few minutes later, an entirely different class was in the room. They were talking and laughing. A few, like Pat, had shed a few tears. They were energized. They were alive. They *believed* their decision to change. They could *feel* their decisions to their very toes. They got it!

The truly exciting part for them and for me, as their teacher, was that they didn't lose that energy. They didn't lose that feeling. Even through difficult money belief changes and difficult money behavior changes, the women were able to remind each other of their inner power and strength. Each of these women could still remember *feeling* the power and the strength of her decision to change.

So if you haven't moved out of your chair yet, maybe you'd be willing to move now. After you get out of your chair, read the change decisions you wrote in your notebook. Read them out loud and with all your emotions: with your strength, with your pain and with your hope.

Keep reading until you *feel* your words all the way down to your toes. When you *feel* it in your toes, you know what empowerment *feels* like. Empowerment is your inner strength — your inner power. You can now *feel* that power. You have both the power and the strength to make changes in your money life.

Now, instead of just hoping you will be able to make changes, you *know* you have the strength and the inner power to make these changes in your money life.

You now know you have the power to *un*learn what you have learned about money.

You now know you have the power to reshape your money belief puzzle pieces and reshape your money behavior puzzle pieces, which you identified in chapter 4. You have the power to reshape these puzzle pieces so they all fit — so you have no more conflict between what you believe and what you are actually experiencing.

You have the strength and the power because you have decided. "No more!"

An empowered woman is a woman who has *felt* her inner strength and power as she makes a change decision about her life. The difference between an empowered woman and a victimized woman is that the empowered woman knows that she has the strength and she knows she has the right to make decisions about her life. An empowered woman has *felt* to her very toes that inner strength and power.

A woman who has never *felt* this strength and power is a victim . . .

- who is scared of making decisions because she doesn't know if she has the right to make a change decision.
- who doesn't know if she is capable of making a change decision.
- who doesn't know if she can trust herself to know what change decisions she wants to make in her life.
- who waits for others to decide for her and hopes she'll be all right.

You are a woman. You have *felt* your strength. You have made a decision to change. You have said, "No more!" You are an empowered woman. It's your life. You get to decide about your life:

- *You get to decide* what you want to do with your life.
- *You get to decide* what is important to you.
- *You get to decide* what doesn't work in your life.
- *You get to decide* what changes you want to make in these unworkable parts in your life.
- *You get to decide* how you want to make changes in your life.
- *You get to decide* with whom you want to make these changes.
- *You get to decide* when you want to make these changes.

As an empowered woman, you're in charge of your life. No one else has the right to tell you what you should or shouldn't do. Or what you're capable of. Or what hurts. Or what gives you pleasure. Or what feels important. Or what feels clear. Or what feels safe. No one else has the right to make change decisions for you. That's your job. You're the adult. It's your life.

Making adult change decisions is sometimes difficult. If these change decisions were easy, you would have already made these decisions to change.

The change decisions that you need to make now are the big decisions, and they are probably going to be a bit difficult.

Change always has a fear component. The fearful part of any change is that you worry that you may end up giving up more than you will actually get when you make the change. As difficult as it is to live with the inner conflict between your childhood learned money beliefs and your life experiences, many times it feels even more difficult to give them up and practice a new way of looking at life — a new way to live. No matter how difficult it is to live with this inner conflict, it still feels harder to try new, unknown beliefs. This is called the *fear of change.*

Most adults become willing to change when they are absolutely convinced that their lives are too difficult and too unworkable the way they are. They feel backed into a corner. They're scared. They're frustrated and tired. They begin to believe that no matter how hard the change might be, it must be better than the present difficulties. They become willing to risk their fear of change and try a new way.

You probably picked this book up because you felt a need to change the way you think about money and the way you act with your money because it isn't working for you. You may be frustrated. You may be scared. You may feel confused. You may feel embarrassment or even shame. Maybe you're just tired of it all.

It's Time To Try Something New

So you say to yourself, maybe, after all these years, it's time to try something else. Maybe, after all these years, it's time to try a new way of thinking about money. Maybe it's time to try new behaviors — a new way of acting with my money.

Let's say every day at 3:15, Christina, my nine-year-old daughter, comes home from school in tears. For the last four years Christina has been attending the same school, walking home the same route and coming home every day in tears. Every day I give her a hug and say, "What happened?" Every day Christina tells me that a mean boy comes out of his house and pushes her and scares her. Every day.

Every day I say to my daughter as I wipe her tears, "It's all right, honey. Maybe tomorrow when you come home, the boy won't bother you and scare you."

Christina, being the smart girl she is, says to me, "But, Mom, he's been scaring me every day this year, and last year and the two years before that. He always scares me."

Now as the mother of this child, do I tell her to keep trying the same route, even though it isn't working and has never worked? Wouldn't I be a rather incompetent mother if I keep telling her to take the same way home, hoping she won't be scared *this* time?

As a caring, competent mother, I will tell my daughter that she needs to find a new route home because her old route isn't safe for her. Her old route home hasn't ever worked and it isn't working now. This new route may have some problems, and when the new problems come up, we will have to deal with them. But we know for sure there are problems with the old route. So it's time to change. And I tell my daughter that she and I will keep experimenting with this change until she absolutely knows she is safe walking home. We will keep trying new routes until she absolutely knows she doesn't have to be scared.

It seems very simple when we are talking about taking care of a child.

Your decision to find a new way — a new route — in your money life can be just as simple.

The conflict between your money beliefs and your adult money experiences is the scary, unsafe route you've been taking in your adult money life. This route has created unworkable financial problems. It's time to make a decision to change your route by changing your money beliefs so you feel safe. It's time to change your route by changing your money behaviors so you can know you really are financially safe. It's time to say, "No more!"

Making a change, even one for the better, will bring new problems. Money change can be hard, and some of the problems that come with this change may seem quite difficult for you. But the present conflict in your money life is also difficult. Your old way of thinking about and acting with your money is not working. Looking for a new way means changing both your beliefs about money and your behaviors with money.

Chapter 6 will help you in your decision to change your learned money *belief* puzzle pieces so your inner-belief conflict can be resolved.

Chapter 7 will help you in your decision to change your learned money *behavior* puzzle pieces — your life experiences.

When your belief puzzle pieces and your behavior puzzle pieces fit, the inner conflict is over. You feel safe. Even though the financial change may be difficult, you feel safe because what you believe fits with what you are experiencing in your money life.

Open your notebook. Read what you wrote in the exercise at the beginning of this chapter. What you are reading is your personal decision to change.

Telling yourself, "No more!" is a decision to change. "No more!" is a decision to be safe.

Telling yourself, "No more!" is the same as telling yourself, "I'm willing to unlearn the old learning that's not working for me."

"I'm willing to risk change."

You can begin your change in the next chapter.

✣ SIX ✣

IT'S MY LIFE.
I GET TO DECIDE.

"It can't be this simple!" Beth was talking. "You mean I can just decide and I'll change? I don't believe it."

Believe it. It really is this simple. By making a decision to change, you are already changing. You made your decision to change in chapter 5. Now it's time to do it.

The mechanism of change is very simple: If you want to change your money life, you need to change your money beliefs — your feelings about money. You also need to change your money behavior, which is the way you act with your money. And if you want to change your money behavior, you begin with the way you think and feel about money — your money beliefs.

Change is simple, but it can also be hard.

"Hard? I can do hard," Beth said, when this came up in class. "For goodness sake, hard is what my entire money life has been so far. Hard and scary and hopeless. Listen, I have been going to my 12-Step recovery group every week for a little over four years now. I have been in weekly therapy for almost three years. I made a decision many

59

months ago to give up acting and thinking like a victim. I decided to give up the scary and hopeless parts of my life. Hard? Treatment was hard. But treatment gave me hope. Recovery has been hard. Recovery is giving me a life."

Beth's voice was shaking as she continued, "I'm so sick of all the crises I have with money. I just can't stand always feeling this fearful hopelessness over my money. Without change in my money life, my recovery isn't really working."

A very determined Beth continued, "Hard? I can do hard. My money life has been hard. Just tell me how to change. I want to feel some hope. I'm ready."

Because behavior can never go beyond beliefs, money behavior will never change without a change in money beliefs. That's why your budgets and money planning have failed in the past. You've tried to make yourself change your money behavior, without changing the way you *think* about money. Changing your money beliefs by developing a new way of thinking about money is absolutely essential.

You have been practicing your learned money beliefs for your entire life. That's a lot of years of practicing thinking about money the way you do. That's why your money beliefs are so strong. All those years of practicing may make your thinking and your feelings about money — your money beliefs — difficult to change.

In order to change, you need to know *what* money beliefs you are changing and *how* to change these money beliefs.

Most of women's money beliefs can be categorized into three core money beliefs. These three money beliefs seem to be universal in our female society and family training. All of the women who have taken my classes over the years have expressed one or more of these three core money beliefs.

Core Belief #1: "I Shouldn't Have To . . ."

"I'll take care of you. Don't you believe me?"

"You don't understand, I shouldn't *have* to." Suzanne's face streaked with tears as she spoke. She was explaining to the other women in the "Women and Money" class that her husband of 17 years had left her. The mother of two teenage boys, she was in the process of divorce.

It sounded like a scenario from a soap opera, but it was real life.

"I worked in an awful job to put that man through school so he could get a good education and be able to support our family. Then I took care of the kids and the house and entertained for his business. In every way, I did what I was supposed to do. Now at the age of 44, I either have to go back and finish my college degree with a bunch of kids in their twenties or find another awful job somewhere. So I either go into debt for school costs or I lock myself into a dead-end job just to pay the bills. It's not fair. I shouldn't have to . . .."

As Suzanne expressed her hurt, other women in the class were nodding their heads. They, too, knew what it was like to feel betrayed. They did what they were taught they were supposed to do. Then the rules changed.

Our culture teaches women they shouldn't have to learn the financial rules for handling money because:

- Someone or something else will be in charge of the money — a husband, a father, God, the Universe.
- Good, lovable women will be taken care of financially and won't end up alone and poor.

Suzanne believed this training, and now her beliefs — "I shouldn't have to . . ." — are in conflict with her life experiences. So what was Suzanne going to do? After receiving much support from the other women with her anger and her fear, Suzanne continued.

"I figure," explained Suzanne to the class, "what do I have to lose? I might as well give up the belief that says someone else will take care of me because it doesn't look like it's true. It's not going to happen. It seems so simple. I'll just have to change my belief. I'm still really angry, though, at how much I have had to hurt before I got it that this money belief is a lie.

"It isn't deciding I'll have to learn about money that scares me," Suzanne continued in a soft voice. "What really scares me — and I'm a little embarrassed to even say this — is that sometimes, even with all this pain, there's still a part of me that wants to believe I don't have to do this. There is still a part of me that wants to believe that someone or something else will take care of me — that this is only a temporary situation.

"Oh, well, I guess all this means is that I may be a little resistant to making this belief change. But believe me, this really hurt, and I will change even if it takes some time. What I'm telling myself is:

> *I shouldn't have to, is a lie.*
> *I do have to learn about money, is the truth."*

Core Belief #2: "I Don't Want To . . ."

"If you don't want to, you don't have to.
Don't you believe me?"

"But I don't *want* to always have to work," said Pat angrily, as she looked around the room. "First, I brought home the money while he finished his business degree. Then he got a job, but we both needed to work so we could pay off the school debts."

Sounding extremely frustrated, Pat continued. "After that, I went back to school to get my Master's degree so I could increase my pay at work. I couldn't quit my job while I was in school because we needed the money for a down payment on a house. We got our house, and three months later the business he worked for went bankrupt. So now he's home soothing his bruised ego and I'm still working."

Pat, a 36-year-old social worker, was talking to the class about her anger and frustration with her career life. This frustration had reached a peak because she had just found out she was pregnant.

"If I didn't have to work because of money, I'd be ecstatic about this pregnancy. I don't want to go to work right now. I want to stay home and be pampered. My mother stayed home with her babies and I want to stay home with mine. Who changed the rules so that I have to work even when I don't want to? My husband is doing odd jobs because he can't find a job. I know it's hard for him, but I don't want to work.

"There's really no way out," she continued. "No matter what happens, I won't be able to stay home and take care of my baby. I thought about asking him to leave, but that wouldn't solve the problem either. I'd still have to earn an income and there'd be no one to help with anything. Besides, I love him. I'm just angry and frustrated because I feel let down and lied to."

Pat was expressing the belief many women share. They feel caught between not *wanting* to always work for an income and knowing they *have* to. This money belief says that women's work for an income is nonessential. Women have been trained to believe that their work for income is only temporary, and they will come and go from their work as their relationships in life change.

The real truth for most women is that work income is very necessary to their lives. As frustrating and difficult as it is to accept sometimes, the real truth is that the world has changed since Pat's mother was able to stay home with her children.

How did Pat change her money belief?

"I went to a friend's house for two days," Pat explained. "The first day I spent most of the time crying because my life hadn't turned out the way I believed it would. Then I stopped crying, and on the second day I said to myself, 'You can spend your life crying, or you can take what you have and make it work.' I decided that since I was working full-time, and my husband wasn't, he could take care of the house during the day and he could take care of me when I got home from work. I wasn't going to work full-time and clean the house and make the meals, too. We'll save enough money so I can stay home for a month when the baby is born and then, if my husband still isn't earning an income, I'll need to go back to full-time work. He can take care of our baby instead of putting the baby in day-care. I'll just have to learn to parent my baby in a different style from my mother."

Pat continued, "When I went home and explained my plan to my husband, he agreed. This plan isn't our first choice, but I really do have to earn an income.

" 'I don't want to . . . ' " Pat told the women in the class, "is true for me, but it doesn't work in my life. The truth is I *have* to work outside the home. So I say to myself:

> *Even if I don't want to. I'm willing to."*

Core Belief #3: "I Can't . . ."

*"So you don't need to try.
Don't you believe me?"*

"What am I supposed to do about this ghastly financial mess I'm in?" an exasperated Jane asked the class. "I feel as if I'm stuck in quicksand and I'm slowly sinking.

"Let me explain. The Internal Revenue Service says I owe them back taxes for three years. How can I possibly owe any taxes? I'm broke! I have an appointment scheduled with some man at the IRS in six days. He told me to bring in all my records, and he'll figure out what I owe in taxes. Records? I don't have any records. I don't even know what he means by records. Isn't someone else supposed to do this tax stuff? The man on the phone from the IRS didn't sound like he wanted to help me much. Do other women know how to do records and pay taxes even when they're broke? I don't even know what I'm supposed to know."

As scared as she sounded, Jane still wasn't finished. "On top of all this, I just got a letter saying my bank is going to close my checking account. The bank says I've bounced too many checks. So what's the problem? I pay them $19 every time I bounce a check. That's a lot of money. I don't see what they're griping about."

Jane's anger quickly disappeared as she fought back tears of frustration. "I really don't know what to do. It feels like I'm in a trap and there's no way out. I want to quit. I just can't do it."

Many of the women in the class who were listening to Jane had also experienced the same sense of being stuck in a financial trap. They understood what it feels like to have financial problems and not know how to solve them. Jane, like other women in the class, was taught that because she was female, she wasn't intelligent enough or competent enough with numbers to *learn* money skills. And Jane, like other women in the class, was taught she wasn't emotionally competent enough to be as disciplined as she needed to be to *practice* the skills of successful money management.

"I'd never thought about this before," Jane continued, "but I remember once telling my parents I was going to become a veterinarian when I went to college. They had a good chuckle over that one. My dad gave me a big hug and said, 'Honey, you don't want to take all those hard science and math classes. You're so cute. Why don't you just marry a veterinarian?' At the time I remember thinking, 'Science and math classes, yuck!' Now I realize they were telling me I wasn't smart enough to get through those classes. I wonder if they were right? I'll never know, will I?

"The problem is," she said sadly, "I've never married, and I was taught that the way I would handle the practical matters of life was by letting a man do them for me. Maybe I've never found anyone who did it as well as my dad. My dad died three years ago, or I could've asked him for help now." Jane paused to listen to what she had just said.

"Say, wait a minute! I've got it all wrong, haven't I?" Now Jane sounded rather excited. "The point was that I was *told* I wasn't smart enough to do all this money stuff

by myself. And I *believed* what I was told. But I really don't
know that for a fact, do I? Maybe I'm really smart. I'll bet
it will be hard and I'll bet I can do it. I can learn at the ripe
old age of 34 how to get out of this financial mess. I tell
myself:

> *I can't is the lie.*
> *I can. Oh, yes, I can is the truth.*
> *It's my life. I get to decide that I can."*

Affirmations

Suzanne, Pat and Jane have each identified a women's
core money belief that has caused them a great deal of
pain. Each woman has made a clear decision not to stay in
her pain, but to find a solution out of that pain — to
change the money belief that was causing the pain.

In order to change the way you think about money —
your money beliefs — you will need to retrain your brain.
Your brain has been conditioned by your money training
that began when you were a little girl. Your brain has
been conditioned to believe things that are not true and
have not worked in your money life. In fact, many of the
ideas and beliefs your brain learned have created real pain
in your adult life. It is time to change these beliefs. It is
time to retrain your brain.

Open your notebook and look back at the writing you
did in chapter 2, "How Did I Get This Way?" This is
where your brain training began. This is the money training you will want to undo by retraining your brain.

Now check what you wrote in your notebook for chapter 3, "Why Is Money So Hard For Me?" These are your
specific money beliefs, the result of the money training
you identified in chapter 2. These are the money beliefs
that you are now going to change.

There are two primary methods of retraining the brain
in order to change money beliefs.

The first primary method of retraining the brain is through *affirmations*. An affirmation is simply a new, positive belief statement. Affirmations use words to retrain the way the brain thinks. Remember in chapter 3, when you identified your personal belief barrier as the words you learned to say to yourself in your money life? Affirmations use *new* words that will retrain the way your brain thinks about money.

To feel the effect of the change power of affirmations in your money belief life, make sure you do two things:

First, you must feel the affirmation in your body when you say the affirmation or when you write it. This means that in order for an affirmation to do its job in retraining your brain, you must feel strong emotion with the affirmation. The brain seems to "listen" better to the new beliefs — the affirmations — when there is feeling with the words.

In order to be able to feel your affirmations, you will want to pick beliefs that are important to *you* to change. You will want to pick beliefs that have caused you a great deal of pain in your life. You will also want to say the affirmations in language that "feels like your language." You won't want to pick language that works for me or for Suzanne or for your friend. You will want *your* language — your words.

Second, in order to feel the changing power of your affirmations, you have to believe the affirmation as you say or write it. Really and truly allow yourself to believe what you are saying — way down to your very toes. If it seems impossible to really believe, I have found that affirmations work even if you have to "cheat" a little. "Cheating" means that you "act as if" you believe what you are saying or writing. "Acting as if" means that you shut your rational, thinking brain off just for a second, and allow yourself to believe, just for the second that you are saying your affirmation, that what you are saying is actually true.

Remember when Jane told the class, "I can. Oh, yes, I can. It's my life. I get to decide I can!" It sounded great. But as soon as Jane stated her new belief — her affirmation — to the class, she turned to me and said, "I really can't, you know. It really is hopeless." And she started to cry.

Even with her tears, I didn't let her back down from her decision to change. I asked her to read, through her tears, her new belief — her affirmation. I asked her to pretend by *"acting as if"* she still believed it. She read, *"I can. Oh, yes, I can. It's my life. I get to decide I can!"* And she read it again. And again. And again. And again.

As she reread and reread, she stopped pretending. Just for those moments, she really believed her affirmation. The entire class could tell by the tone of her voice and the way she held her body that she really believed her affirmation.

Affirmations need to be repeated many times a day for many, many, many days. They need to be repeated until the brain really believes these new beliefs to be true.

Remember how you felt in the last chapter, as you walked around the room and said, "No more . . .?" "No more . . ." is an affirmation of change. Remember how strong and clear you felt? You're already changing!

Continue your change with the title of this chapter. Use this title to help you practice both the *feeling* and the *believing* of new money beliefs — of your affirmations. Say to yourself out loud, *"It's my life! I get to decide."* Say it again, with feeling way down in your gut. Again. Now, again. Believe what you are saying and feeling. It *is* your life. You *do* get to decide. Say it again: *"It's my life. I get to decide."* Say it over and over as you feel and believe what you are saying.

How do you feel? Do you feel energized? Empowered? Strong? Focused? Confident?

How do *you* feel? What are *your* words? In your notebook, write the words you are feeling. _____

Now let's go to work and specifically change some of your old, unworkable, painful money beliefs.

Turn back in your notebook to the writing you did for chapter 3, "Why Is Money So Hard For Me?" This is the chapter where you identified your belief puzzle pieces — the ones that don't fit and are creating conflict and pain in your life.

Look at the list where you identified your money training and then you identified your resulting money belief. It's time to reshape your belief puzzle pieces.

In your notebook, first list the old, adult money belief. Just pick any one on your list from chapter 3.

My old money belief: _____

_____

Now *decide* what you would like to believe in order to feel the way you felt just a minute ago as you said, "It's my life! I get to decide." Remember the feelings of empowerment and strength and confidence?
What do you *affirm* as your *new* adult money belief?

_____

_____

If you're a bit stuck with the language of affirmations, let's check in with some of the women you read about in chapter 3. These are some of the changes the women made in their old money beliefs.

Pam's *old belief* was: "I'm not smart enough."
Pam's *affirmation* is: *"I know I'm very, very smart. Plenty smart enough to do money."*

Joanne's *old belief* was: "I could never handle money."
Joanne's *affirmation* is: *"I'm really good with my money. Really good."*

Sara's *old belief* was: "I'm a compulsive overspender. I can't trust myself. I have no discipline."
Sara's *affirmation* is: *"I can trust myself."*

Do you get the idea of the language of affirmations?

Beth's *affirmation* is: *"I have a great calculator and I'm really good with numbers."*

Kathryn's *affirmation* is: *"I am decisive and clear."*

Mari's *affirmation* is: *"I'm in charge of my money. Yes, I am!"*

Judy's *affirmation* is: *"Married or single, I'm an incredibly smart money manager."*

Again, using your notebook, you are going to reshape *all* of your old money belief puzzle pieces that you listed in chapter 3. You will do this by restating each of your old adult money beliefs, and then changing each of those old beliefs to your new, adult money beliefs — *your affirmations of change.*

My old money belief: _____

_____

My affirmation of change: _____

_____

How about another one?

My old money belief: _____

_____

My affirmation of change: _____

_____

Another?

Keep going until you have *affirmed a new, empowered money belief* for each of the old money beliefs. Keep going until all of the old beliefs have new powerful words of change.

Now, in your notebook, make a clean, clear list of your new powerful words of change — your affirmations:

1. _____

_____

2. _____

_____

3. _____

_____

4. _____
   _____

5. _____
   _____

Congratulations! You're changing. Let's keep going.

Visualization

The second primary method of changing your money beliefs is by using *visualization*. Affirmations use *words* to change beliefs by retraining the brain. Visualizations use *pictures* to change beliefs by retraining the brain.

In order to make these new beliefs really work, it's important to retrain the brain with both words and pictures. The combination of words and pictures is quite powerful.

Visualization is practicing success by *picturing* yourself as successful. Visualization is a mental pictorial rehearsal of empowerment, of confidence, of competence, of strength and of commitment. You need visualized rehearsal so that you are ready for the real thing: lifetime money success.

Visualization describes a new picture of you as you would appear to yourself and to others with all your affirmations — your new money beliefs — as a part of your life. This picture is how you see yourself and how others see you as you live your life with your new adult money beliefs.

> I am independent, powerful and happy. Wow! I'm quite a woman. Hello world. Here comes Beth.
>
> *Beth*

> I am caring, giving and rich. Yeah, rich! I am considered to be very astute with money. Really smart. I am on many social change committees that I feel strongly about. I am able to give a lot of money for what I value. I feel great!
>
> *Joanne*

> I am a wonderful role model for my daughters as they see me learn all about money. I am even making my own

investments! I feel successful with money and I feel successful as a mother.

Pat

I am a strong, independent, successful woman. I am listened to at work. My family respects my opinions. I feel beautiful in my own style. I feel good about who I am.

Mari

Now it's your turn. Open your notebook to a clean page. On this blank page, write a description of this new you with all your new money beliefs. Write a description of this empowered, strong, clear, successful woman. Picture in your mind how you act, talk, look and feel. Picture how others respond to you. Visualize this new you and write your visualization on the page in your notebook.

⚓ SEVEN ⚓

SOMEDAY IS HERE.

Remember how you've said, "*Someday* I'm going to live within a budget?" Or, "*Someday* I'm going to get disciplined enough to make a budget work." Or, "*Someday* I'm going to have a budget that lasts more than one payday." Or, "*Someday* I'm . . .?"

Well, guess what? *Someday is here!*

"You mean now?" a voice says, clearly in shock. "Right now?" This is a common reaction in the "Women and Money" classes when I begin to teach the skills of budgeting.

"But we haven't had enough time to practice our affirmations and visualizations," the voice protests. "We need more time before we start working with budgets."

"Remember," I tell the class, "your affirmations and visualizations are changing your old unworkable money beliefs to new empowering money beliefs. You are changing these old money beliefs so you can change your money behavior. Affirmations are never a substitute for action. Learning and practicing new financial behavior is the action. The purpose of affirmations and visualizations is to *allow* you to learn new financial behaviors."

"But," the voice from the class continues, "budgets are so boring and constricting and complicated and rigid. They never work anyway."

Maybe this voice sounds like your voice. Maybe you too have a lot of resistance to learning about budgeting. Many women do. You associate pain with the word budget — or the "B" word, as some class members so fondly refer to budgeting — and you may resist. You may be remembering all the feelings of failure you have experienced in the past when you have attempted to budget and the budget hasn't worked.

The resistance you may be feeling is simply a response to your past experiences with budgeting. Since you are an intelligent and competent woman, you understandably resist repeating past failure and pain.

Remember?

"I shouldn't have to . . ."

"I don't want to . . ."

"I can't . . ."

These old money beliefs haven't worked for you. Right? These old money beliefs have caused your past budgets to result in failure and pain.

That's why you have decided to retrain your brain. You've written new beliefs, which are your affirmations, so you can begin to retrain how you think about money — your money beliefs.

Budgeting is simply the next step. Budgeting retrains your *behavior* with money.

This may be a good time to open your notebook to the list of affirmations that you wrote in chapter 6. These affirmations are a list of your *new* money beliefs. You may want to read them out loud to yourself right now:

"I have to . . ."

"I'm willing to . . ."

"I can. Oh yes, I can . . ."

All the way through this chapter, you will want to tell yourself over and over: "I have to . . . I'm willing to . . . I can . . . I have to . . . I'm willing to . . . I can . . . I can . . . I can. Oh yes, I can." Keep propped up in front of you the page in your notebook that has the clear clean list of your new money beliefs — your affirmations. Whenever you feel fear or frustration or hopelessness, *or* you hear yourself saying, "I don't have to do this . . . I can't do this," immediately read out loud your list of affirmations.

Or sit quietly and read out loud the visualization you wrote. Picture *you* in your mind as you read. Picture this strong, clear, successful, hopeful, empowered, recovering woman. *You.* This is the picture of the you that said, *"Someday* I'll become."

Someday is here.

There are two basic skills to budgeting. No, these skills are *not* buying a new calculator or buying new batteries for the calculator or becoming smarter or liking numbers more or being better at algebra or getting a raise or . . . all of the other ideas you may have of what budgeting is.

Again, there are two basic skills to budgeting. Without these two skills, budgets always fail. Your past budgets have failed for two reasons:

- *Reason Number 1:* Your old money beliefs have stopped you from changing your money behavior, so your past budgets have failed. Remember: The way you act with your money — your money behavior — cannot change before you change the way you think about your money — your money beliefs. Your money behavior can *never, ever* go beyond your money beliefs, which are the ways you think about money. You already know this because of the work you did in chapter 6.
- *Reason Number 2:* You haven't learned the two basic skills of budgeting.

It's as simple as that!

First we'll identify these two budgeting skills so that you can understand what they are and how they work. Then, in the next chapter, you'll set up your own practice budget. The budget will give you the chance to practice and learn these two new budgeting skills.

Budgeting Skill #1: Setting Financial Boundaries

A *boundary* is a limit, a place that you stop yourself, a line you don't cross.

A *boundary system* is a series of boundaries.

A *budget* is a boundary system.

Stop for a moment and think about all the boundaries that are part of your life that you just take for granted:

- Closing the front door of your apartment or house.
- Locking the front door.
- Driving your car into the garage.
- Locking the car doors or rolling up the windows.
- Driving on the right side of the middle line in the road in this country, or on the left side of the middle line of the road if you are driving in Europe.
- Closing the refrigerator door.
- Sleeping in your bed and eating at the kitchen table rather than vice versa.

See, you do know how to set and keep boundaries. These are all examples of boundaries at which you are quite skillful.

You've learned more difficult boundaries, too. You've learned boundaries in your job. You've learned when you are to be at work and when you are to go to lunch. You've learned what is appropriate to wear to work and what language is expected. You've also learned the political and social boundaries concerning what you say to whom and when.

You've also learned more difficult boundaries in your personal relationships. You've learned when you are to be available to each other and when you are to be separate. You've learned who does what to provide the food that you eat together. You've learned boundaries concerning monogamous agreements the two of you have made together.

Even though some of these boundaries are more difficult, and you may not feel as if you are always as skillful at setting and keeping some of these boundaries, you still know you need to have boundaries in work and relationships.

You're also learning boundaries in your recovery — boundaries with yourself and boundaries with others. As part of your recovery, you continually practice setting and keeping these boundaries.

Many of you were raised in family systems with little or sometimes *no* healthy boundary role-modeling. Healthy boundary teaching did not take place in any part of your life — not in relationships, not in jobs and certainly not in money, or you wouldn't be reading this book. No one taught you by their actions and their words how to set and keep boundaries with your money. Because of this, when you've tried to set and keep healthy, safe, financial boundaries, many times you have met with failure.

If you add this lack of healthy role-modeling of financial boundaries to your *women's* financial training which says, "I shouldn't have to . . .," "I don't want to . . .," "I can't . . ." — you can see why you've met failure when you've tried in the past to budget:

- You have met failure in budgeting because you have *never* been shown or told *how* to set and keep healthy boundaries with money.
- You've been told you *don't have* to learn boundaries with money and you're *not capable* of learning anyway.

Pretty incredible, right? Given this kind of boundary training, no wonder you've had a problem! Can you imagine if you had this same kind of training in all the other areas of boundary setting? Can you even imagine how difficult your life would be?

You're now bringing money into your recovery. You're deciding you can and, in fact, need to learn healthy boundaries with money, just as you've learned and are learning them in other areas of your life. This book can serve as a role model for you on how to set these financial boundaries. When it gets hard, you have your affirmations propped up in front of you to remind you that you *can* learn this skill and that you are *willing* to learn.

Budgeting Skill #2: Estimating And Predicting

"What if I bought that Barbie outfit and that big box of Legos, *then what?"* seven-year-old Jenny asked her mother.

"If that's more money than I have from my allowance, *what if* I bought that Barbie outfit and that little box of Legos? *What would happen then?"* she continued.

"If that's still too much money, *what if* I bought the small box of Legos and that jump rope? *Then what? Would* I have any money left over? *What if* I saved the money that's left over and kept it until I get my allowance next week? *Then* could I get the Barbie outfit, too? Or *would* I have to wait until I get two more weeks of my allowance?"

"What if . . .?"

"Then what . . .?"

"What if . . .?"

"Then what . . .?"

Seven-year-old Jenny is learning the second basic skill of successful budgeting. She's learning what questions she needs to ask so she can understand the consequences of the money decisions she's making. She's learning to budget. She's learning what questions she needs to ask so she can . . .

- get what she wants *and*
- *not* get herself into financial trouble

Jenny is learning what questions she needs to ask so she can get the toys she wants *and* have enough money to pay for them when she gets to the cash register.

In order for seven-year-old Jenny to learn what questions to ask, she needs someone who will help her learn. She needs a parent who will patiently take the time to help her understand how to balance what she wants to buy with what she has available to spend. She needs a parent to teach her how to get what she wants in a way that won't hurt her.

Seven-year-old Jenny had a parent who was helping her learn the skills of *estimating and predicting the consequences* of her money decisions.

"I feel so jealous," Diane interrupted in one of the "Women and Money" classes. Tears were coming unchecked down her cheeks as she continued. "Oh, I wish I were Jenny. Oh, I wish I had someone who cared about me like that. Who was kind and patient. Who took the time. Who didn't shame me."

Diane's eyes snapped as she went on. "I'm angry! I'm very angry I got cheated out of my rightful parenting. I'm really angry at my parents. It's not fair. I should've learned all this when I was little. They should've taught me."

Like Diane and many other women reading this book, you may not have had a parent who taught you the skills of money management — of budgeting. You may not have had parents who helped you practice the skill of *estimating* what it is that you want and need, and at the same time helped you practice the skill of *predicting the consequences* of those wants and needs.

Like other women reading this book, you may not have had parents who taught you to ask the money questions: *"What if . . .?" "Then what . . .?"*

Your parents couldn't teach what they didn't know.

Because your parents couldn't and didn't teach you these two basic money skills, you may feel anger, sadness, blame, grief, resentment, rage, hopelessness. You may feel these painful emotions as you realize that you were not taught useful money skills. You may feel painful emotions as you realize the price you've paid because you were not taught money skills.

And then you will want to choose to move on. You, as a recovering woman, will want to move beyond anger, hopelessness or whatever painful emotion you are feeling. Letting go of blame and anger means you are moving on in your life. It means you are letting go of resentment and hopelessness as an empowered adult. Moving on means giving yourself permission to learn the money skills you're lacking. Moving on means deciding to parent yourself so you can get what you want and need in your life without hurting yourself.

You may want to take a look at the affirmations that you have propped up in front of you. Look at the one that says, "It's my life. I get to decide." It's true. It *is* your life and you *do* get to decide.

If you are deciding to be successful in budgeting, which is the boundary system for getting what you want and need, you're going to want to give yourself permission to learn the skill of estimating and predicting the consequences. If you're going to learn this skill, you must be taught this skill. If you don't have a parent like Jenny has to teach you, you'll want to teach yourself. You'll want to be your own parent, whether you are seven or seventy years old.

Let's say you've decided to be your own parent and teach yourself the skills of *estimating* and *predicting consequences.*

As your own parent, you'll need to teach yourself the skill of being a responsible adult with your money and still get what the child part of you wants.

As your own parent, you'll need to teach yourself how to take care of your personal finances so you don't get into financial trouble, and:

- still take care of the little girl inside you who wants toys and pretty clothes.
- still take care of the little girl inside you who wants to play and have fun.

As your own parent, you'll need to teach yourself how to *estimate* your wants and needs by asking, "*What if . . .?*"

As your own parent, you'll need to teach yourself how to *predict the consequences* of the money decisions by asking. "*Then what . . .?*"

Estimating and predicting the consequences of money decisions is the second basic skill of budgeting.

Do you remember the serious financial consequences that you identified in chapter 4, "No Matter What I Do, It Doesn't Work"? Look back at what you wrote. Those financial consequences are a direct result of not having these two skills as part of your money life.

In my experience as a teacher, I have found that the hurtful financial consequences women face in their lives are caused by the lack of these two basic money skills: the lack of boundary-setting skills and the lack of being able to estimate and predict the consequences of money decisions. Whether it is with the money that women earn or with the money that women spend or with both the earning and the spending of money, the money problems are there because these two money skills are *not* there.

Because of this lack of useful money skills and because of the resulting money problems, many women label themselves as bad, stupid, hopeless or incompetent, or as too emotional, out of control or compulsive. Many women feel shame and guilt over the amount of money they earn, and shame and guilt about the way they spend their money. Because of the lack of these two basic money skills, most women don't even know when their spending is useful and reasonable and when their spending is harmful to them. None of this confusion or pain or failure or shame or guilt has to be. All this confusion, pain, failure, shame and guilt exist because women are missing these two basic money skills: boundary setting and estimating and predicting the consequences of their decisions. Women are missing these skills because they were not taught these skills.

This is frustrating, but it is also hopeful. You *can* learn these skills. Not someday — right now!

❧ EIGHT ❧

THIS IS A BUDGET?

It's time to learn the skills of boundary setting with your money. It's time to learn the skills of estimating and predicting the consequences of your use of money. In other words, it's time to learn the skills of budgeting.

In order to learn the skills of budgeting, all you have to do is:

1. Be willing to keep your affirmations and visualizations in front of you as a way of reminding yourself not to slip back into your old way of thinking.
2. Be willing to follow, step-by-step, the budget model.
   - Even if it seems uncomfortable — all change is uncomfortable at the beginning.
   - Even if it is confusing — all change feels confusing at first.
   - Even if it's scary — all change is a bit scary when the change is still new.
   - Even if it seems difficult — all change is difficult until you figure it out and get used to the new skills.
3. Be willing to practice, practice, practice!

For this practice, open your notebook to a new page. You may want the register from the checkbook you are using right now to help you remember how you spent your money. If you have them, you may also want last year's checkbook registers or the checks the bank returned to you. A small calculator will make some of the work easier.

Again, keep your affirmations propped up in front of you so you can continue to remind yourself of your new money beliefs.

Before you can practice your new money skills of *boundary setting* and your new skills of *estimating* and *predicting*, you will need to write down some money information. Think of this stage as an informational interview with yourself. You are asking yourself to make lists of information about your money life. That's all. There is no decision making or skill practicing yet. Without judgment or shame, you are just going to write down a clear picture of your money life.

Financial Information: My Money Life

Step 1: Monthly (Fixed) Expenses

Make a list of all your *monthly* bills — the ones that you have to pay each month. These basic monthly expenses are called your *fixed expenses*. They usually cost the same or almost the same each month. You will need three pieces of information about each of these expenses:

1. What is the expense?
2. What is the amount of the expense? (How much do you have to pay or do you usually pay each month?)
3. What is the day of each month that this payment is due?

Monthly (Fixed) Expenses

Name Of The Expense	Amount	Due Date
1. Rent/Mortgage	$_____	_____
2. Phone service	$_____	_____
3. Long distance phone	$_____	_____
4. Monthly utilities: *electric*	$_____	_____
5. Monthly utilities: _____	$_____	_____
6. Loan payment: car	$_____	_____
7. Loan payment: _____	$_____	_____
8. Credit card pymt: _____	$_____	_____
9. Credit card pymt: _____	$_____	_____
10. _____	$_____	_____
11. _____	$_____	_____
12. _____	$_____	_____
13. Therapy: group or individual	$_____	_____
14. Routine/monthly medical	$_____	_____
15. _____	$_____	_____

TOTAL AMOUNT OF PAYMENTS: $_____

Step 2: Yearly Expenses

Make a list of all the expenses you *have to pay* each *year*. These are the expenses that are *not* routine monthly expenses. You may have to pay these expenses quarterly or twice a year or yearly. An example is a car insurance premium that needs to be paid twice a year.

You will also want to list the expenses you *know* you are going to have to pay sometime. You just don't know *when* you will have to pay these expenses and you don't always know exactly *how much* the expense will be. An example of this kind of expense is car repair. You know your car is going to need work sometime, you just don't know when or how much. Another example is an expense for the plumber to fix a water leak or a dental expense.

The best way to estimate these expenses is to look back in your checkbook from last year and see how much you paid. You can also talk to someone who may have more information about the expense. If we are talking about a car expense, you may want to ask your auto mechanic to estimate what your car will need in repair and maintenance for the year. Then you just make your best estimate or guess and write that number in your budget.

Step 2 may be more difficult to figure than Step 1, so keep your list of affirmations in front of you. You *can* do this. Remind yourself again that you have done many difficult things in your life and you can do this, too.

Remember, the money estimates do *not* have to be perfect. Figure them out as close as you can. Your list will be fine.

These expense items are the items that are so easy to forget or pretend aren't going to happen. If you are going to have a budget that is workable and successful, it's important to include in this budget a list of these expenses. Not only do these expenses surprise many of my clients because they have forgotten about them, but many times these expenses can be large. A car repair bill can be quite large; so can a life insurance premium. It's important to include these expenses because you really don't have a choice about paying them. When one of these bills is due, it absolutely has to be paid. For example, when your car insurance comes due, it has to be paid or you don't drive your car.

You will need the same three pieces of information you needed in Step 1, except that the amount of the expense needs to be for the *entire year*. This means if car insurance costs you $350 every six months, write in $350 x 2 = $700. So in the column marked Yearly Amount, you will write in $700.

Yearly Expenses

Expense	Yearly Amount	Due Date
1. Car insurance	$_____	_____
2. License plates	$_____	_____
3. Car oil changes	$_____	_____
4. Car repair	$_____	_____
5. Rental insurance	$_____	_____
6. Tax preparation	$_____	_____
7. Non-insurance: medical	$_____	_____
8. Non-insurance: dental	$_____	_____
9. Home/apartment repair	$_____	_____
10. Life insurance	$_____	_____
11. Non-routine therapy	$_____	_____
12. _____	$_____	_____
13. _____	$_____	_____
14. _____	$_____	_____
15. Unplanned emergency	$_____	_____

TOTAL YEARLY EXPENSE-COST: $_____

Before you are done with this step, you will want to change this yearly cost to a monthly cost so you can "save" money each month to pay these expenses when they need to be paid. Otherwise you may not have the money when these expenses come due and then you will think *you* have failed in budgeting again.

You can make this yearly cost a monthly expense by dividing the above number by 12 for the 12 months in the year. So, if the Total Yearly Expense-Cost was $1,800 a year, this is the way it looks: $1,800 divided by 12 = $150, making the monthly expense $150 to pay for all these yearly costs.

Now it's your turn to do this figuring:

Total Yearly Expense-Cost $_____ Divided By 12 Equals $_____ Monthly Expense-Cost.

Step 3: Total Monthly And Yearly Costs

Now add Step 1 and Step 2 together. Adding these two numbers together will give you your total monthly cost for all monthly and yearly necessary expenses:

Total monthly fixed expenses: $ _____

added to

Total yearly costs divided by 12: $_____

equals

Total monthly and yearly costs: $ _____

How are you doing?

Does your calculator need new batteries yet?

Are your affirmations still propped up in front of you?

Step 4: Flexible Expenses

Now make a list of all the other expenses that this budget is missing. These are the daily, weekly and monthly expenses that are absolutely necessary, but you have more choice in these expenses. You have choice about *what, when* and *how much money you* will spend on these items. In budgeting language, these expenses are called your *flexible expenses.*

You will need two pieces of information for these items:

1. The name of the expense.
2. An estimate or a guess at how much you spend each month for each item of expense.

Flexible Expenses

Expense	Monthly Estimated Amount
1. Groceries	$
2. Eating at restaurants	$
3. Household miscellaneous	$
4. Personal care items	$
5. Lunches at work	$
6. Gifts	$
7. Magazines/tapes/books	$
8. Car gas/bus fare/parking fees	$
9. Entertainment	$
10. Clothing/shoes/nylons	$
11. Dry cleaners	$
12. Holidays/retreats	$
13. Donations	$
14. Hair care	$
15. _____	$
16. _____	$
17. _____	$
18. _____	$
TOTAL MONTHLY FLEXIBLE COST:	$

Step 5: Total Monthly Expenses

Add *Step 3* and *Step 4* together for a new grand total of monthly expenses.

Step 3 monthly fixed expenses: $ _____

added to

Step 4 monthly flexible expenses: $ _____

equals

Grand total expenses: $ _____

Good work with your expenses!

Now in Step 6 you're going to need some income information about yourself.

Step 6: Monthly Net Income

What amount of money do you have available *monthly* for your use? This should be your *net/take-home/spendable income* from your job or jobs, child support, investment income, rental income, alimony. Make a list of your total, spendable monthly income.

Source Of Money	Monthly Amount
1. Paycheck	$ _____
2. _____	$ _____
3. _____	$ _____
4. _____	$ _____
5. _____	$ _____
TOTAL MONTHLY NET INCOME:	$ _____

Step 7: What's Left?

Step 7: Now subtract your *total monthly expenses* from your *total monthly income.*

Total monthly income: $_____

minus

Total monthly expenses: $_____

equals

Plus or minus: $_____

Congratulations! The financial informational interview with yourself is over. You have completed listing your financial information. This information gives you a picture of your personal money life.

Now you are going to use this personal money information to practice the two basic skills of budgeting: the skill of boundary setting and the skill of estimating and predicting.

Setting Up The Practice Budget: Making The Numbers Work

What do I mean by "making the numbers work?"

"Making the numbers work" means that the amount of money that you have available to spend balances with the amount of money you need to pay all your expenses — both your fixed expenses and your flexible expenses. "Making the numbers work" means that you have worked with the numbers in your practice budget so that you have enough money to pay for all these expenses and you don't run short of money. "Making the numbers work" means that you have set money boundaries and you have estimated spending and predicted the consequences of that spending so that you know you have enough money to pay for all your bills and expenses this week, this month and all year.

Are you ready? All right, let's make the numbers in your budget work.

Look back at the last numbers you wrote in your notebook. Do you see where you wrote the amount of money you have available to spend each month? And from that number, you subtracted the amount of total fixed and flexible expenses. This final number will be one of three possibilities.

The Bottom Number Is A Zero

First — and this is the easiest — that bottom number may be a zero. In other words, you are spending exactly what you have available to spend. If you are pleased with your lifestyle and you don't want to make any changes in this lifestyle, you don't *need* to make any changes because your expenses match your income in this practice budget. So you're done with this part of making a practice budget. You're done with this part because we are working on making the numbers work, and your numbers in this practice budget do work.

The Bottom Number Is A Plus Number

Second — and this is the most fun — that bottom number may be a plus number. In other words, you have more money available to spend than what you've said you need for your expenses. If this is true for you, you may want to increase your expenses in three possible areas.

1. If you are in debt to credit cards, bank loans, car loans or any other form of debt, you may decide to increase your payments to your debt. You may decide to double or triple the payment you are making to your bank card. To do this, go back to the first sheet of your practice budget and increase the payment to whatever debt you have decided to pay off faster. Write this new payment into your list of fixed expenses.

2. You may want to start a savings or a checking account for expense items that are not in this budget. For example, one expense item that is not in this budget is vacation. Another item is house furnishings. Another expense item may be seasonal clothing purchases or the expenses of major holidays. If you want to start a savings or a checking account for these larger pleasure items, make a list of all the items that are not in this present budget that you would like to have in your budget. Esti-

mate how much you think you want and need to spend each year on each of these items. Add them together. Now divide the total amount by 12 to make the yearly figure into a monthly fixed-budget amount. Remember how you figured the non-monthly necessary expense items? You will calculate the amount for this pleasure account in the same way.

Now add this monthly amount to your list of fixed monthly expenses. Each month you will deposit this amount in either a checking account or a savings account. When you go on your vacation or buy that new lamp, you will withdraw the money from this special account to pay for that item.

3. You may want to start a savings account just to save. This account is not for the purpose of spending on anything. Money that you deposit into this account just sits in this account so you can feel financially secure. It is *not* for spending on car insurance or a vacation or a new coat. It just sits in this account and looks pretty. After you have enough money in this account and feel wonderfully secure, you will want to transfer some of this money to an investment, so your money can earn more interest than it will earn in this savings account. Right now, though, you don't need to be concerned about *when* to invest this money or in *what* to invest. Right now, you are deciding to save money just to feel safe and secure.

If you have decided to save money in a savings account, write the amount that you plan to save in the fixed monthly-expense list.

Now that you have written the additional numbers into your fixed monthly list, add up all the numbers again. Go all the way through your entire budget to the very last page. "Making the numbers work," which is what you are doing right now, means that the bottom number is a zero. Keep working with your numbers until the bottom number is a zero. A zero means that you have planned your expenses to balance with your income.

Once the bottom number is zero, you may, if you choose, move onto the next chapter.

The Bottom Number Is A Minus Number

Third — and this is the most difficult — the bottom number may be a minus number. A minus number means that your expenses are greater than the amount of money you have available to spend each month. A minus number means that you may struggle to get your bills paid each month. A minus number means that the car insurance bill may upset you when it comes in the mail. A minus number means you may often be discouraged as you try to figure out just how you're going to manage to pay a bill. A minus number means you're probably in trouble with money. A minus number means the numbers in your practice budget are *not* working and you need to make them work.

You have a lot of company from other women as you try to make these numbers work. Most of the women reading this book are in the same place you are right now. Their budget numbers don't work either.

Balancing a budget by making the numbers work is a very simple job. Either you *increase* your income — the money you have available to spend — or you *decrease* your expenses — the money you are spending — or you do a little of both.

Making the numbers work when the bottom line of your budget is a minus is a simple but oh, so difficult job. But you've done difficult jobs before, and you can do this difficult job, too.

First, is there any way you can increase your income? Can you do this without hurting yourself? Is there anything you can do to bring in some additional money that will either get rid of the minus or at least reduce it a bit? What would it be? How much money would it add to your monthly income? How soon can you start?

Next, go through your practice budget. Start right at the beginning on the first page. Is there any way you can reduce the expenses? For example, can you reduce your electric bill by turning off the lights when you go out of the room? Item by item, go through *all* of your lists of expenses. Take your time. Find ways to reduce the expenses in your practice budget.

Now re-total the budget figures, both the new income figures and the new expense figures. If your new ending figure is a zero, you are done. If, like most women working on this right now, you still have a minus, keep working. You have to make the numbers work or you are setting yourself up to fail. You've had enough failure. This time you're going to succeed — even if it is difficult.

Come on! You can do it. Look at those affirmations propped up in front of you. You *have* to do this. You've tried it the other way, and there is too much pain in the failure.

Let's go through it again. Is there anything you can do — to earn more money? Is there anyone you can talk with to brainstorm ideas for making more money? Who? When will you talk to her or him? Any other ideas? Even on a temporary basis? Can you rent a room to someone? Do you need to ask for a raise at work? Or raise your fees if you are self-employed? Does your child-support money need to be brought current or increased? Does anyone owe you money that you need to collect? How about a garage sale? How about a part-time sales job?

There must be a way to increase the money you have available to you. What can you do?

Now let's go through your expenses and do the same kind of brainstorming. Is there any way to lower the cost of your groceries? Can you shop at a less expensive grocery store? Can you write menus to reduce the food waste? What can you do to lower your grocery costs?

Is there any way to lower the cost of your therapy without hurting your therapy process? Can you go into a therapy group to reduce the cost of individual therapy? Can you reduce any other of your medical expenses?

Do you really need those magazines and newspapers? Do you really need to spend that amount on laundry and dry cleaning? Or on clothes? Or entertainment?

Come on! You said this was important to you. Where can you make changes? Can you negotiate with your landlord to paint the apartment or mow the lawn yourself so the rent can be reduced? Maybe you can't afford to live where you are. Do you need to move? Can you get a monthly bus pass to lower your bus costs? Can you increase the deductible on your car insurance so your premiums go down?

Please don't give up! Please keep working with the money figures until the bottom line is a zero. You owe it to yourself to succeed. You owe it to yourself to feel smart and competent and empowered. Keep brainstorming. Keep adding and subtracting. Call a friend and brainstorm.

Keep working the money figures until the bottom number is zero. Then you know you have made the numbers work. Making the numbers work is necessary to the success of your new practice budget.

This is a budget? Yes, this is a budget!

When you have made the numbers work, you know you have a working budget on paper. Yes, this *is* a budget. This is *your* practice budget.

You've done it. Look back at the pages in your notebook. Do you see all the signs of the struggle you have been through? Do you see the erasures, the crossed out numbers, the torn paper, the broken lead, the dried tears?

Congratulations!

You have used your creativity, your persistence, your downright stubbornness, your hope, your intelligence and your determination to create a budget with numbers that really work.

You have *set money boundaries* in this budget. You have *estimated* your needs and wants as you have also *predicted the consequences* of these estimations. You have been practicing the two basic skills of budgeting. You really *are* learning new money skills.

Most people who actually get the numbers to work on paper stop at this point. They think that magically the budget will jump off the paper and become part of their lives. But it doesn't work that way. After all this work, the budget just sits on the paper and becomes another failure system.

So please — don't stop here. Your next step is to take charge and make this budget come alive.

Take charge and make this practice budget work in your daily life.

❧ NINE ❧

I'M IN CHARGE.
YES, I AM.

Can you imagine how different your life would be if you could say with absolute surety, "I'm in charge of my money. Yes, I am. No doubt about it?"

Can you imagine the difference *within* yourself as you go about your life? Can you imagine the *inner* sense of empowerment you would feel — the *inner* sense of safety and prosperity you would feel?

And can you imagine how your **outer** life would be different — the clarity and confidence with money decisions, the ease of bill paying, the look of prosperity?

All of these changes are possible. All it takes is a commitment to change both your money beliefs and your money behavior. This commitment affirms your decision to change the way you think about your money. This commitment affirms your decision to change the way you behave with your money by learning the two new money skills of boundary setting and estimating and predicting

the consequences of your money behavior. This commitment affirms your decision to follow a concrete money
plan that will hold you accountable to yourself as you
practice these new money skills.

In chapter 5, "No More!" you made a decision to change
your money beliefs and your money behavior.

In chapter 6, "It's My Life. I Get To Decide," you began
to support the decision you made to change your money
life by deciding to change your money beliefs, which are
the ways you think about your money. You did this by
writing new empowering affirmations and by creating a
visualization of yourself and your new money behaviors.

In chapter 7, "Someday Is Here," you began the process
of changing your money behavior by identifying the two
specific skills you are lacking in your money life.

In chapter 8, "This Is A Budget?" you continued to
support this beginning process of change in your money
behavior by writing clear, specific money information in
your notebook. Because of this information, you now
have a balanced budget in your notebook. The numbers
in your budget work.

But you're not done yet. The budget you have written
in your notebook is not in a workable form. The budget
is just sitting there. No matter how easy or how difficult
it was for you to get your budget numbers on paper and
working, the budget still is not an active part of your life.

A budget, *any* budget, creates a place for you to practice
the two money skills: the skill of boundary setting and the
skill of estimating your wants and needs and predicting
the consequences of that estimating. Your budget has the
capability of providing continual growth in creating a
sense of financial ease — both now and when you are
older. Your budget has the capability of creating a sense of
confidence and competence and a sense of financial clarity.
It has the capability of creating a sense of financial success
and prosperity and creating a sense of empowerment.

So what's missing?

"What do I still need to do," you may ask, "to make my
budget a workable part of my life?"

You need a firm commitment to learning the two basic money skills. You also need a concrete plan that allows you an accountable place to practice these new skills.

"But I already made that commitment," you may say. "And I have a plan — a budget that I just balanced."

That's true. But in order to make this budget a living part of your life and give yourself an accountable place to practice these new money skills, you will want to develop a very specific money plan. This very specific plan is called a *Self-Contract*. This contract with yourself answers basic questions you will want to ask yourself in order to make this budget an active part of your life. You will want to ask yourself:

- *What* am I going to do?
- *When* am I going to do it?
- *How* will I know that I have done it?

Remember seven-year-old Jenny, who is learning to ask the questions, "What if . . .? Then what . . .?" By learning to ask herself these two questions, Jenny is learning the basic money skills of estimating and predicting the consequences of that estimating. Jenny is learning how to make appropriate money decisions based on the amount of money she has. She is also learning when she needs to be clearer about what things really cost. She is learning when she has "done good" as she makes her choices.

Many women simply don't know when they've "done good." Many women were never taught how to know when they are making useful decisions and when they are making hurtful decisions with their money. Perhaps, like many women, you were never taught when your money choices were appropriate and when they were not appropriate. You were never taught in a way that you *really* know when you are succeeding in your money decisions and when you are making a mistake.

In order for learning to be successful, the learner needs to have a clear way to measure progress, to identify when the learning is working.

In order for learning to be successful, the learner also needs to have a clear way to identify mistakes — to identify when something isn't working, so you can make adjustments in what you are doing instead of giving up — to keep learning instead of feeling you have failed.

The Personal Self-Contract

A personal Self-Contract will be able to give you this clarity.

Your personal Self-Contract is a concrete plan in which you hold yourself accountable for specific actions, at specific times, in order to give yourself a place to successfully practice the new money skills. Your personal Self-Contract is a measurable commitment to change in your money life. Your personal Self-Contract will tell you the truth about yourself as you ask: "Am I doing *what* I said I would do in my money life? Am I doing it *when* I said I would do it? Is it working?"

Your personal Self-Contract is an action plan you make for yourself in order to practice your new money beliefs and your two new money behavior skills. Your personal Self-Contract changes your budget from a flat listing of numbers on a piece of paper to a working, viable part of your life.

If you are willing to make a clear commitment to change in your money behavior, it's time to write a personal Self-Contract.

If you are willing to make this commitment by writing a Self-Contract, it won't be long before you will be able to say with surety, "I'm in charge of my money. Yes, I am."

Before you begin to write your personal Self-Contract, I want to tell you something that a personal Self-Contract is *not*. A personal Self-Contract is *not* a perfection agreement. There is no such thing as perfection in recovery. There is no such thing as perfection in learning new money skills. There is no such thing as perfection in life. Rather than perfection, there is growth and learning and progress. There is gentleness in the face of mistakes.

There is celebration in the face of success. A personal Self-Contract is a clear, concrete agreement with which you can practice learning from your mistakes and practice celebrating your progress.

Are you ready?

Writing A Self-Contract

If you are ready, open your notebook to a clean sheet of paper. At the top of the sheet, write *My Personal Self-Contract.*

Your Self-Contract will list at least *five* agreements with yourself. These five agreements will answer the questions:

- *What* have I decided to do to support my commitment to change?
- *When* will I do what I have said I will do?
- *How* will I know I have done what I said I would do when I said I would do it?

First Self-Contract Agreement

In order to keep your commitment to changing your money beliefs, you will want to make your affirmations a part of your daily life. These are the affirmations that you have had propped up in front of you since you wrote them in chapter 6, "It's My Life. I Get To Decide." These affirmations need to become firmly ingrained in your brain because changing your old money beliefs to these new money beliefs is the basis of any money behavior changes you want to make. Remember? Your Self-Contract will not succeed unless these affirmations are at the base of this commitment.

In order to make affirmations part of your daily life so they can become firmly ingrained in your brain, I suggest you make a commitment to write them in your notebook as part of your morning routine *and* as part of your evening routine. Writing them in your notebook twice a day will become part of your daily routine, just like brushing your teeth or combing your hair. I suggest you write *each* of them *five* times — morning and evening. As you write them, say them out loud to yourself.

Deciding to write your affirmations in the morning and in the evening is the setting of a boundary. Setting a boundary is the first money skill. Deciding to write them five times in the morning and five times in the evening is the skill of estimating the number of times you need to write your affirmations in order to learn these new money beliefs. As you write your affirmations, you are predicting your success in learning new money beliefs. This estimating and predicting is the second money skill.

I suggest you also carry a copy of these affirmations in your billfold. Maybe put a copy of them on your refrigerator. Maybe put a copy of these affirmations on every doorway in your house. How about in the front of your appointment book? Or on your desk or taped to the inside of a drawer at work?

Surround yourself with your new money beliefs. You are reprogramming your brain. Post them wherever you can, so you don't allow yourself to forget them.

If you are willing to make a commitment to writing your affirmations in the morning and in the evening at least five times, write the commitment down in your notebook on the page that says: *My Personal Self-Contract.*

First Agreement:

"I am willing to write my affirmations in the morning and evening at least five times."

As part of this first agreement, write down *where* you will keep copies of your affirmations — in your house, in your billfold, in your office and so on.

"I am willing to . . ."

Also, after writing your affirmations in the morning and in the evening, will you make a commitment to take a moment and form your new picture of you — your visualization of yourself? If you are, write:

"I am also willing to . . ."

Congratulations! You have made a commitment to your personal Self-Contract *first* agreement.

This *first* Self-Contract agreement allows you to make your new money beliefs a part of your daily life.

Second Self-Contract Agreement

Now, you will want to make the practice budget from chapter 8, "This Is A Budget?" a part of your daily life. You will want to find a way to get your budget off those sheets of notebook paper and make it an active part of your daily decision-making. You will want to make your budget a useful practice tool for learning the two basic money skills you identified in chapter 7. For this, I suggest you establish some clear, concrete rules for the money in your budget. You will need to answer these three questions with these rules:

- *What* do I need to do with my money?
- *When* do I need to do it?
- *How* do I know I have done what I said I need to do with my money?

In order to answer these three questions, you will want to set some money rules. This *second* Self-Contract agreement has *five money rules.*

Rule #1: Deposit All Money

You will deposit all money that is available to you to spend in your personal checkbook. This money may be from your paycheck, your income from a small business, your child-support, your investment income, your retirement income, your Social Security, your alimony or maintenance. It may be money earned in a garage sale or at a part-time job. Wherever the money comes from, you will want to deposit all of it into your personal checking account.

Rule #2: Fixed Expense Checks Only

The *only* checks you will write from this personal checkbook are the expenses you have listed in the *fixed* expense lists in your budget. These lists are the *first two* budgeting lists that you wrote down in chapter 8. Remember, these two lists of expenses are the necessary expenses that you pay monthly. They are also the *necessary* expenses that you know you have to pay quarterly, twice a year and yearly. These expenses are also the emergency *necessary* expenses, such as car or home repairs.

Again, the only checks you write from this account have to be on one of the first two budget lists you made — the necessary and the fixed bills.

Rule #3: Flexible Expense Cash Salary For The Week

One day *each week*, you will write a check to "cash." This is your *cash salary for the week*. This cash salary is to pay for *all* of the expenses in your budget that we called *flexible* expenses. These are the expenses that you have more choice in when you spend your money and how much money you spend. In order to figure out how much money you will have each week for these expenses, take the monthly number for all these flexible expenses and divide that number by 4.32. (You'll want to use the number 4.32 for the number of weeks in a month. A month is not a perfect four weeks long. Each month is almost four and one-third weeks. When you want to change a monthly expense amount to a weekly expense amount, you need to divide the monthly expense amount by 4.32.)

On your calculator punch in the total cost of all the flexible expenses for each month. Then punch the divide sign. Then punch in 4.32 and then the equal sign. The number on the screen of your calculator is the amount of money you will write a check for each week to pay for all the expenses that are on the list that says flexible expenses.

For example, if your total flexible expense budget for the month is $385, you will divide $385 by 4.32 and the number on the screen is $89 each week for your cash salary. Or if your total flexible expense budget is, say, $900 each month, you will divide $900 by 4.32 and the number on the screen is $208 for each week's cash salary.

This rule sometimes sounds difficult and confusing but it is very, very important because it is the only way to answer the question, "*How* will I know if I am spending the amount of money I said I would be spending on groceries and eating out, paper products and gifts for myself and for others . . . and all the other things that I usually spend more on than I said I would?"

This rule is very, very important because it allows you to be successful. If instead of this rule, you write down everything as you spend it, how will you know if you have spent too much? If instead of this rule, you add up at the end of each week all that you spent that week, how will you know *how much money you have to spend when you are actually spending your money?* How will you know if you have stayed within your budget or not? What if Jenny's parent had said to her, "Just buy it, and you can figure out when you get home if there was enough money?" It wouldn't work, would it? It isn't clear enough at the time you are making the choices — *at the time you are spending your money.* This rule allows you to know clearly when you are spending what you said you would spend for a particular expense. This rule allows you to know immediately if you are following your budget or if you are going to make a mistake. This rule helps you know when you are successful with your money commitment — when you've "done good."

Use the actual cash each week so you will have real bills and coins for your spending. Actual cash is concrete and clear. When you are out of money, you're done spending. When you have cash remaining, you can still make choices with your money.

Using actual cash will create some logistical problems. If you need to be reimbursed for an item or if the item is a tax deduction, you will want to ask for a receipt and keep the receipt in an envelope in your billfold. But logistical problems, I believe, are a small price to pay in order to change your money behavior. If you doubt that statement, look back to chapter 4 and review the financial consequences of your old money behavior.

Using actual cash will slow you down some in your spending. Whenever you set a new boundary, the new boundary slows you down until you are used to living within the boundary. All this means is that, whenever you set a new boundary, you will want to be fully conscious and fully thinking so you don't break that boundary. That's part of the learning process of new boundary setting, which is the first basic money skill you are learning.

Using actual cash for your flexible expenses will allow you to practice the second money skill. It will allow you to clearly and concretely learn to estimate and predict the consequences of your spending.

"If I eat out tonight, I may not have enough cash to get my hair cut tomorrow."

"If I buy that blouse, I may not have enough money to fill my gas tank."

See how simple it is?

"If I spend this much on groceries, I won't be able to buy that gift for my daughter."

"If I save $20 from this week's cash salary, I will have enough next week to buy those shoes."

"If I buy these groceries, I can invite my group to dinner and still have enough for that book I want to buy."

Making a commitment to paying for your flexible expenses with a weekly cash-salary allows you to concretely practice *both* of the two basic money skills. Making a commitment to using a cash salary for your flexible expenses answers the question, "How do I know I am doing what I said I would be doing? How do I know I am spending the money I said I would spend on these flexible expenses?"

Rule #4: Regular Cash Salary — Same Amount, Same Day

You will give yourself the *same amount of money* each week on the *same day* of each week. In other words, your cash salary, just like your salary at work, doesn't change from week to week. And, just like your payday at work, your cash salary payday doesn't change either. You can pick any day you want. You can decide. But you will want to keep it the same every week. This rule answers the questions: *What* amount of money do I have available to spend? *When* do I have that money to spend? *How* do I know if the money is enough? *How* do I know if I have enough money for that item? *How* do I know my budget is working?

Rule #5: Eliminate All Other Spending Tools

During this time when you are practicing new money skills, I suggest you make an agreement with yourself to stop using all of the other spending tools you have available to you. This means you will use for spending *only* your personal checkbook and your cash salary. This means that you will put away, cut up, seal up or freeze in a gallon container your bank cards and your cash cards. This means you will stop using lay-bys, lines of credit, Ready Reserve and whatever other spending tools you have used in your money life.

In chapter 8 you developed a budget that balances. You found a way to make the numbers work: The amount of money you have available to spend balances with the amount of money you said you needed for your expenses. That was clear. In this new money behavior system, you will be paying all your necessary, fixed expenses out of your checkbook. You will be paying all of your flexible expenses out of your weekly cash salary.

You are following this rule so that you can practice the skills of boundary setting. You are also practicing the skills of estimating and predicting the consequences of your money decisions. In order to practice these skills, you need to be clear with your money.

All the other spending tools create confusion in your money life: "How much money do I really have? Can I afford to buy this or can't I? I don't know. I think so but I'm not sure . . ."

These other spending tools create denial: "If I don't have the money, I can always charge it." Or, "If I don't have enough money in my checkbook, I'll just go more into my Ready Reserve."

Neither confusion nor denial can have a part in your new, prosperous, clear, recovering money behavior.

Let's keep it simple. Either you have the money or you don't. If you don't have the money, you may ask yourself, "What am I going to do to live and be well until I pay myself my next cash salary?" If you do have the money, you may ask yourself, "Is this really the way I want to spend my money? It's my money. How am I going to decide how to spend my money?"

All right, it's your turn. I have listed five rules that I believe are important to making your practice budget a part of your daily life. Are you willing to make a commitment to keep these five rules as the second agreement in your personal Self-Contract?

If you aren't, go back to chapter 3 and 4. Read to yourself what you wrote in your notebook for these two chapters about your unworkable and many times quite painful money beliefs and your money behavior. Now read what you wrote in your notebook for chapter 5 of this book. Read how you said "No more" to these old money beliefs and hurtful money behaviors. Now read and reread your affirmations that you have propped up in front of you on your cards.

It *is* time, isn't it? It *is* time to learn new skills so that your money life doesn't have to be so frustrating — so hurtful. No one ever promised that learning new skills is fun or easy. But learning new skills and seeing the change those skills are bringing to your money life is so very hopeful. It *is* time.

Again, are you ready to make a commitment to the five rules for this second agreement? If you are, write in your notebook:

Second Agreement:
"I am willing to keep the five money rules."

Now, so you know *exactly* what you are going to do and when you are going to do it, write down what the above agreement means for each of the five money rules:

Rule #1: *I will* deposit all of my money into my checkbook.

Rule #2: *I will* only use my checkbook for the fixed and necessary bills. Since I don't need my checkbook for daily living expenses, *I will* leave my checkbook at home with my expense bills.

Rule #3: *I will* pay myself $_____ (amount of money) each week in cash and no more.

Rule #4: *I will* pay myself this cash salary each week on _____ (day of the week).

Rule #5: *I will* stop using all other spending tools except my checkbook for my fixed and necessary bills and my cash salary for my flexible living expenses. *I will* . . . (write down what you will do specifically with each spending tool. For example, I will put my Visa card in my safety deposit box. I will cut up my Master-Card and send it back to the company. I will not use lay-bys . . .)

Congratulations! You have made a commitment to your personal SELF-CONTRACT *second* agreement.

This *second* agreement allows you to practice the two basic money skills so you can see change in your money behavior.

Third Self-Contract Agreement

For a third agreement with yourself, I suggest you schedule a business meeting with yourself once a week. Sounds interesting, right? You will want to do this as an internal monitoring system so that you can get used to being accountable to yourself in your money life.

I recommend that you write in your appointment book or on your calendar a time during the week when you are willing to sit down with yourself and focus on your money. In addition to keeping yourself accountable, this business meeting will do two things for you:

1. If you are meeting with yourself once per week, you start to begin to *trust yourself* with your money. You will begin to trust that you really do have a working commitment to make changes in your money life. "Look at me," you will say to yourself. "I really am getting the bills paid, the checkbook balanced, the creditors called, the car insurance mailed on time. I really am getting all these things done."

If you are meeting with yourself once a week, you will start to develop the skills of financial clarity as you learn to trust yourself with the financial tasks.

2. If you are meeting with yourself once a week, there's no need to worry about your money at two in the morning or on your break at work. You can start to *defer* money worries to this business meeting. You don't have to think about your car insurance at four in the morning or during the evening meal because you know you will handle the car insurance at your next business meeting.

I recommend you schedule no more than an hour each week, and you may only need a half hour. But the time needs to be written in pen in your appointment book or on your calendar. So unless you are in an ambulance on the way to the emergency room, you will be meeting with yourself at that time. This business meeting with yourself is that important in your money life.

You may want to experiment with different times during the week that would work for this business meeting. You don't want to be exhausted or it will be easy to give up and not have your meeting. You don't want to be taking care of children or you will be too fragmented. You won't want to answer your door or your phone. If someone wants to see you or talk with you at the time of your scheduled business meeting with yourself, tell them no. You may say to them, "I'm sorry, but I'm unavailable at that time. I have a business meeting scheduled."

You can find a time for this meeting. Even with all your other commitments, you can *make* time for *you*. You make time for others, now you can make time for something you have said is very important to *you*.

You will also want to set an *agenda* for this meeting. Otherwise, when you really do sit down with yourself, you won't know what to do and you may feel discouraged. The *first thing* you may decide to do at your business meeting is to go through your weekly schedule and plan what cash you will need for each day of the week. It may be helpful to actually bring your weekly cash salary to the business meeting. As you go through the weekly schedule, you can make little stacks of money for all the flexible expenses. You have decided to do this so you absolutely *know* that you will be all right with your money during the week.

If you're supposed to meet a friend on Thursday, make sure you put the money that you will need for Thursday in a little stack. You can just tuck it away until Thursday. If it's your friend's birthday, make sure you have cash tucked away for a gift. If you need groceries or a tank of gas or a haircut, tuck the money away. Do you see how you are making this budget work?

The *second thing* you may decide to do at your business meeting is set a specific financial task. You may want to set a different task for each week of the month. Make sure you bring the checkbook and your bills to this meeting so you can complete each task.

The *first week of the month* you may decide to reconcile your checkbook or bring your checkbook into the bank to be reconciled.

The *second week of the month* you may decide to pay all your bills that are due in the middle to the end of the month.

The *third week of the month* you may decide to make calls that need to be made — to creditors, to the insurance agent, to your financial planner, to your bank and so on.

The *fourth week of the month* you may decide to pay all your bills that are due at the beginning of the month.

See how you can plan these weekly financial tasks so that it works?

After these tasks are done, your business meeting is done. The meeting is over for the week. These meetings can be so simple, yet they have such a high payoff. You will learn to trust yourself with your money.

Are you willing to make a commitment to a weekly business meeting as your third agreement? If you are, write in your notebook:

Third Agreement:
"I am willing to have a weekly business meeting with myself. I am willing to meet at _____ (time of the day) on _____ (day of the week) in _____ (place)."

Congratulations! You have made a commitment in your personal SELF-CONTRACT to a *third* agreement.

This *third* agreement teaches you accountability to your skill building. This accountability is part of the money behavior changes you said you want in your life.

Fourth Self-Contract Agreement

Change can be difficult. If change were easy, you would have already made the changes you need to make in your money life. You would have made them without this book. Change also is a process and it takes time. During this difficult, time-consuming period in your life, you will need support.

This book can serve as a model for your change, but it doesn't give you enough support. You need more support than this book. The purpose of support is to keep you accountable in your learning process. The purpose of support is to celebrate your successes. Support can also help you brainstorm ideas when you are stuck, discouraged and don't know what to do next.

There are several ways and places you can get support:

1. Give a friend a copy of your contract with yourself. Ask your friend to check in with you about your money changes and be willing to celebrate your successes and brainstorm when you're stuck.
2. Invite one to five other women to read this book as a group. You can decide to meet every week or every other week. If you are going to get support in this way, you will want to make sure all the women have as strong a commitment as you to really making money changes in their lives. Make sure this group doesn't become an "ain't it awful" group. The women in an "ain't it awful" group will spend their time talking about how discouraged and stuck and hopeless they feel. Discouragement is not the purpose of this group of yours. The purpose is to give support and help and hope as you role-model change and growth for each other. If you use *How To Turn Your Money Life Around* as a guide and focus, a group of women such as this can be a wonderfully strong support in your process of change.
3. Use your individual and/or group therapy as a support. Be sure to talk with your therapy group about the commitment you have made to yourself and specifically ask for support from your therapist.
4. Use the 12 Steps and your 12-Step recovery group to get support. You may want to report what your commitment is and what happened. Keep it simple, short and clear. Your 12-Step recovery group can be a very committed and clear support as you change.

Are you willing to make a commitment to getting support for the money agreements you are making with yourself? Decide whom you will ask to give you support and decide when you will ask. If you are willing, write in your notebook:

Fourth Agreement:
"I am willing to get support."

Then, finish this sentence:

"Specifically, these are the ways I will get this support. I will . . ."

Congratulations! You have made a commitment in your personal SELF-CONTRACT to a *fourth* agreement.

This *fourth* agreement is for the purpose of keeping you accountable — of celebrating your successes and not giving up when it gets hard.

Fifth Self-Contract Agreement

Your life is important. Your change is important. Your growth is important. Your learning is important. But the uniqueness of change and growth and learning is that when you learn what it is that you're practicing to learn, you forget the time when you didn't know what you know now. When you have growth in your life, it's hard to remember how you felt and acted before your growth. When you change, it's hard to remember what your life was like before your change.

Do you remember when you learned to read? It's hard to remember the process of pronouncing each sound in each word, isn't it? You may remember where you learned to read, but it's difficult to remember how clever and how smart you felt as you learned the basic phonics of reading.

Do you remember when you learned to ride a bike? Do you remember the frustration of falling and the courage it took to get back on the bike to try again? Do you remember how strong you felt when you cycled all by yourself to the end of the block and back again?

Do you remember how impossible it seemed to try to steer the car and work the gas pedal and maybe even work a shift and a clutch when you learned to drive a car? Do you remember how important and adult you felt when you drove to the store for the first time all by yourself? It was like a rite of passage.

"Now that you mention it," you may say, "I do remember how those changes felt. I had forgotten."

I'll bet that right now you are feeling quite good about yourself because you allowed yourself to remember the feelings of strength and cleverness you had when you learned these skills, even though it was probably many years ago. You allowed yourself to remember the successes you had in your growth and change.

Part of my job as a teacher is to help the women in my classes to remember what they have learned. It is to help them remember the feelings of helplessness *before* they made the change and the feelings of empowerment during the process of change. Part of my job is to remind the women how far they have come and how much they have learned. It is to remind them how courageous and competent they have shown themselves to be as they have grown and changed. Showing themselves how clever and smart they are helps the learning process.

Knowing there has been progress even though everything isn't working perfectly gives hope to continue the progress. Knowing how courageous they have been in the past gives courage to the women in the class for the present. Knowing how smart they were in the past shows them they are just as smart or smarter now.

Remembering the process of growth, any growth, makes the growth visible and real. Remembering the process of growth in money beliefs and money behaviors makes the financial growth real to each woman. She sees that she has made progress even though her budget is not working exactly the way she wants. She sees her progress even though she makes mistakes with her cash. She sees her progress even though she still has a lot of old debt. She sees her progress and she knows she is changing and growing. This knowledge gives her hope for the future and confidence in the process of her financial change.

Remembering the process of growth reminds each woman in the class of the feelings she had as she changed and grew. When she is feeling helpless because she just broke one of the rules in her personal Self-Contract, she remembers how courageous she felt when she wrote the contract and she willingly tries again. When she is feeling stupid because she over drew her checking account because of an error in her subtracting, she remembers how smart she felt when she balanced her budget and made the numbers work.

As your teacher, I can't do for you what I do for the women in the classes. I can't help you remember your growth and change process and the emotions that go with this change. And yet, as an important part of your process of change, you will want to allow yourself to remember. Acting as your own teacher, you can allow yourself to record your process of growth and change and record the emotions you felt as you were growing and changing.

So, in your fifth Self-Contract agreement, I am asking you to take my place and be your own teacher. I am asking you to agree to record your growth and change. Recording your financial growth and change means that you will agree to keep a journal of your change process. This is a daily journal in which you can write a little or a lot. You will want to write about your feelings because this will record the growth in your money beliefs. You will want to write about your actions with your money each day because this will record the growth in your money behaviors.

Whenever you get discouraged and think you aren't changing or you can't change because the change is taking too long or is too hard, you will want to spend a few minutes and read in your journal. Reading in your journal will help you remember the courage you have shown in your money changes. Reading your journal will show you how smart you are and how far you have come in developing new money skills.

If you are willing to make a commitment to recording in a journal your personal process of financial growth and change, write in your notebook:

Fifth Agreement
"I am willing to write in my journal every day. I will use ___ _____ (what notebook?) as my journal. I will write in the _____ (morning or evening or both)."

Congratulations! You have made a commitment in your personal SELF-CONTRACT to a *fifth* agreement.

This *fifth* Self-Contract agreement allows you to be your own teacher as you remember all that you have learned and empower yourself in your own living-growth process of financial change.

Take a deep breath. You did it. You're done!

You have written an agreement with yourself that makes your practice budget an active part of your daily life. You have written an agreement with yourself that clearly — without confusion or denial — states your new recovering money behaviors. You have written an agreement with yourself that answers the three questions:

- *What* have I decided to do to support my commitment to change?
- *When* will I do what I have said I will do?
- *How* will I know I have done what I said I would do when I said I would do it?

Now all that stands between you and successful, empowering money beliefs and money behaviors is *practice*. Just like when you learned to read or ride a bike or drive a car, it took practice. And more practice. And more practice. This personal Self-Contract allows you clear, workable guidelines for practicing your new money beliefs and your new money behaviors.

So, practice. Be patient with yourself, follow the agreements you made in the Self-Contract and practice. It works!

✥ TEN ✥

IT'S WORKING!

"It's working," Janet said to me and to the "Women and Money" class as she walked across the room to a chair. "It's really working!"

Janet provided the opening for the final meeting of the class. I looked around the room at the 14 women and I remembered the fears, the pain and the struggles they had expressed during the earlier classes. Now I saw 14 talking, laughing, confident, capable, smart, courageous and persevering women.

The change I saw in these women is what makes being a teacher so exciting. It isn't as if all their money problems are over — far from it. It isn't as if they all of a sudden keep their personal Self-Contract rules perfectly — far from it. It isn't as if they never become discouraged and frustrated — far from it.

The change I saw in these women is that now they *know* they can do it. Each of these women absolutely *knows* that she has made changes in her money life — both in how she thinks about her money and how she acts with her money. And she absolutely *knows* she will continue this growth process of change. She absolutely *knows* her money life will only get better and better. Each of these women is starting to understand what true empowerment really means. She is starting to understand the vast capacity of her inner strength and power to make financial changes even when it is very, very difficult.

But wait a minute. I might as well let them tell you what they are experiencing. I will let these women model for you their sense of empowerment. I will let them give you ideas to help you find solutions to problem areas you may be having in your new money life. Maybe they can inspire you to continue to believe in your living process of growth and change in your money life.

Janet's Story

"Ruth," Janet addressed me, but looked around at the rest of the class, too. "I've made so many budgets and none of them ever worked. I never could figure out what to do to make a budget work. And then whenever my budget would fail, I would say to myself, 'See, you screwed up again. You'll never get this right.'

"I feel sad," Janet said in a quiet voice. "Ever since I was a little kid, I haven't been able to figure out when I was good and when I was bad. I'd think I was being good, and all of a sudden someone would hit me. So then I knew I had been bad. I understand now that getting hit wasn't about whether I was good or bad, but was about my alcoholic father and his abuse. I decided as a kid I could never learn the rules well enough. I'd never learn the rules well enough to be really safe so I wouldn't get hit."

In a low voice, Janet told us, "I've really hurt myself with money. I haven't known how to get my bills paid and still have something left for myself. When a creditor would call, I would feel like I had just been hit by my dad. I knew I had been bad, but I didn't know what to do to not have it happen again.

"But now it's working. All my bills are paid for this month," Janet said in a more animated voice. "I even have some cash salary left from last week and I think I'm quite wonderful. Do you know I'm even putting some money in a savings account? Not bad, huh? Not bad, especially considering I am absolutely the champion of failed budgets."

Denise's Story

"Oh, no, you're not," Denise interrupted Janet. "If there's going to be a contest for the greatest number of failed budgets, I win hands down."

"Sorry, Janet," Denise continued with a chuckle, "for taking this wonderful honor away from you. Not only could I win a contest for the most failed budgets, but I'll bet I could win a contest for blowing each failed budget by the widest margin in the shortest amount of time.

"You see, when I used to plan my budgets, I would get really hard-nosed with myself," Denise explained. "I think I used to look on my budgets as a form of penance for all my overspending between this budget and the last budget. I would tell myself, 'Denise, you've messed up so horribly, now you have to pay for it.' Then, because I'd feel ashamed, I would make promises to myself. I'd put these promises into a budget. In my budget I'd decide to make payments on all my bills. By the time I'd pay all my bills, there never was any money left for me. So I'd promise myself that I wouldn't go out to eat with my friends. I'd promise myself I'd bring my lunch to work, I wouldn't buy any clothes and I could wait to get my hair cut.

"The amazing part of all these promises," Denise told the other women in the class, "is that each time I wrote down a budget, I really and truly believed I would be able to make all those payments. I really and truly thought I would — this time — live without all my pleasures. And for a while I would. I'd be very disciplined for a while. I'd pay my bills. I'd shop for groceries with a list and coupons. I'd stay away from the malls. See, I really do know how to do this budgeting. But it always felt so hard to do.

"And then," Denise bluntly admitted, "I'd blow it. Sometimes I had been disciplined for a whole payday, and sometimes I'd been disciplined for just a few hours. But then I'd blow it. When I was going to blow it, I'd tell myself, 'Denise, you are a 42-year-old professional with a good job. You deserve to buy this.' Or I'd say to myself, 'It isn't fair you can't go out with your friends. It'll all work out. You'll get your bills paid. Don't worry.' So I'd spend the money. Then I'd feel ashamed because I really thought I'd keep my budget this time. I just didn't know how to work with myself to take care of me and get my bills paid at the same time. Like Janet, I didn't know how to make my budgets work so I'd feel good about myself.

"But, no more!" Denise exclaimed. "No more! My budget is working. I'm not using my credit cards. A friend of mine, Jan, is holding the two cards I decided to keep. Anytime I leave the house, I have in my purse my cash for the week and — hang on to your chairs — a newly opened checkbook just to buy my pleasures. I don't have very much money in that account, but the money that's in it is only for pleasures. So now when I meet a friend for lunch, I first check my cash to see what I can afford. Then if I don't have the cash, I look in my checkbook to see if I want to part with the money in my checkbook to pay for the lunch. Yesterday I had lunch with my friend, Jan, and all I ordered was a cup of coffee. Can you believe it? I'm really getting cheap. I ate the sandwich I made for lunch in the car on the way to the restaurant. I saw an outfit at the mall that I want. So I'm saving the money in my checkbook to get the outfit. I'm thrilled! It's working. All my bills are paid, and I'm not charging. I'm actually saving money to buy things."

Mari's Story

"I'm saving, too," Mari interjected. "I've never been able to save in my life. Travel is what I've always wanted to do. I've always had money automatically deposited from my paycheck into a travel savings account at my credit union to pay for trips. But I never could keep the money in that account. I always needed the money for something else. When it would be time to go on the trip, I had no money. So I would charge all the expenses for the trip. Last time I did that, it took me over two years just to pay off one trip. It was awful.

"But it's different now," Mari continued. "I'm going to brag a bit. I think I need to hear myself brag because I'm still in shock that at the age of 48, for the first time in my life, I have a trip paid before I go. This is how I did it. I still have money automatically deposited in my travel fund, even though I lowered the amount because I needed more money in my checkbook to pay the bills. And even though it is a smaller amount, it's all there. Amazingly, I haven't spent any of the money. When emergencies have come up, I've had enough money in my checkbook to pay for them. I have a trip to Greece planned in two months. Can you believe it! Romantic Greece! I've always wanted to go to Greece and now I'm going. And I won't need to charge even one penny for the trip. Which means I can start to plan my next trip as soon as I get back from this one. I can hardly believe it myself. The money in my savings account will pay for all airfare and lodging costs.

"But I must tell you the most amazing part," Mari said excitedly. "All of the spending money I will need for this trip I saved out of my weekly cash salary. Amazing! I give myself $120 per week for all of my non-bill expenses. Out of this cash, I pay for my haircuts. I found a place that charged less than half what I was paying. I pay for my car gas and I pump it now myself.

"Oh, I know," she laughed, "all the rest of you have probably been doing this for years. But, hey, some of us are a little slower to catch up.

"But anyway," she continued, "I want to keep bragging. I bring my own lunch which I eat with my friends at the cafeteria at work. And, well, to make a long story short, I was spending less on many things. Then I found out that spending less on these things didn't necessarily mean I was able to save any money. I just found other things to spend the money on, like a new blouse or a good book. I really wanted to save money for this trip, so I started experimenting to try to trick myself not to spend. I had been taking my cash out in 20-dollar bills. I just spent it all. Then I took the cash out in two 50s and a 20. I found it hard to cash the 50s. I know it probably seems silly to you, but a 50-dollar bill seemed so large that I didn't want to break it. I'd do anything not to have to break that last 50-dollar bill each week. I got very, very cheap. And — ta-da-da-da — I am going to Greece on my 50-dollar bills from my weekly cash salary." And with that, Mari stood up and took a bow to the cheers of the women in the class.

Jane's Story

"I find it quite amazing how real those bills and coins are," Jane spoke up. You probably remember Jane because of her problems with her bank and the IRS. "If you can save to go to Greece, Mari, maybe I can save, too. I've never taken a trip that I paid for, ever. Because I haven't paid for the trip, I've never had a say in where we were going on the trip. Or at least I've never been asked my opinion and never felt I should offer it. I'd really like to be able to help decide where we'll go for a trip and to have the money to pay for my part of the trip. If you can do it, maybe I can, too. I give myself $90 each week for my cash salary. I'm going to see how much of that money I can save this week. Then I'm going to put that money in a jar that has a sign that says 'Trip Fund.' I wonder where I would like to travel? As I'm deciding, I can watch my money jar get full of cash for the trip. Just think, a jar full of cash."

Beth's Story

"There is something so great about having this cash," Beth interjected. "What is it about this cash? You know, Ruth, I ignored your advice when we first started the cash salary agreement. I did set a weekly amount of money for my cash salary goal. But it was just a goal. I still used my checkbook and a charge card. I also used some cash. I tried to keep track of how close to my goal I was. Some weeks I would go over my goal, and some weeks I would go under my cash goal for the week. But it wasn't working. The problem was I wasn't accumulating enough money in my checkbook for the non-monthly expenses or for emergencies. My car insurance premium came due and I didn't have enough money in my checkbook. First I got mad. I thought, 'Right, Ruth. This budget sure works great. I can't even pay my bills.' I told a friend that the budget I learned in this "Women and Money" class wasn't working. Knowing that I like to go my own way with things, she asked me if I was sure I was following all the suggested rules for the budget. The only rule I wasn't following was the rule about using the actual cash. She strongly suggested I give the budget rules an honest try and use the cash. I made an agreement with her that I would.

"So," Beth continued, "I left my checkbook and credit cards at home and withdrew from my bank account the cash for the first week. Well, the first week I was so scared I would run out of money and be stranded somewhere without my checkbook, I actually had money left over. The second week, I not only spent all of the left-over money I had from the first week's cash, but I also spent my entire second week's cash salary by the third day of that week. I couldn't believe it. I called my friend and told her it didn't work and I would need to get more cash. She challenged me to try to make do until my next cash salary payday. And I did! I really did it! Something changed within me when I got my cash for that third week. I remember looking at my little stack of cash and wanting to protect it. For the first time in my life, my money had real value. I realized how important that little stash of cash was to my life, and I realized I would need to be very careful how I spent my cash. I don't know how to explain the change in me," Beth continued with a little awe in her voice, "but I felt all different about me and my money.

"I'm 34 years old, and I never really got it that this is my money and I need to be careful and make good choices or I won't be able to pay my bills and buy my food. I really am becoming quite cheap and it's fun. That's the part that's so amazing. It was fun to hear what Mari did to get to Greece and it's fun to think about what I want to do with my money."

Joanne's Story

"It's fun for me just to know that I won't spend $130 this month on overdraft charges in my checkbook," said Joanne. "I've tried every way possible to get myself to reconcile that checkbook and just can't do it. Sometimes when I would try to sit down with it, I would actually feel sick. But then I would get sicker when the overdraft notices started to come in. I thought of having my husband do it for me, but I knew I would probably never hear the end of it. Besides, I was too ashamed to show it to anyone, including him. Then I remembered, Ruth, how you said that someone at the bank could do it for me. I also remembered that you said, 'No matter how muddled your checkbook is, the person at the bank has seen worse. I promise.'

"Well, to make a long story short, I went into my bank and I just left my checkbook with the woman. I didn't even want to watch. I picked up my checkbook later that day. She charged me only $15 for all that work. I now have a balance in my checkbook that she believes is accurate. The woman at the bank suggested I bring my checkbook back next month just to make sure the balance is really accurate. I told her I would. Then do you know what I did? I asked her if next month she would show me how to reconcile the account. I want to be able to do this myself. Not bad, huh?"

Joanne was interrupted by shouts of "Terrific!" "That's great!" "Good for you!" The other women in the class were truly excited by Joanne's growth and change. She and Jane had seemed the most stuck at the beginning of the class. And Joanne had been very quiet during many of the class meetings.

Joanne got tears in her eyes as she listened to the support. Then she laughed out loud as she told the women, "Never in a million years did I ever think I would be cheered for not having overdrafts in my checkbook." Then she looked very serious again, "Actually, I never in a million years thought I would get cheered for anything. Thank you."

Judy's Story

The class got quiet again as Judy started to talk. "I took your advice, Ruth, and wrote letters to all my creditors. I was going to call them, but I just didn't have the courage. So I wrote letters instead. But before I promised them how much money I would send them, I did what you suggested and I figured out my budget so I would have enough money to pay my monthly bills and my non-monthly bills and to pay for any emergencies. The big change for me was that I also made sure I kept enough of my money to pay myself a cash salary each week. I set an amount that seems to be workable, which means I can live pretty well without feeling so deprived.

"When I feel deprived, I just blow the whole budget. Then I don't get my payments in and then my creditors call me. Then, like Janet, I feel like I'm a bad person. Like Janet, I didn't learn how to set the rules so I could know when I was good — not bad. I didn't learn how to set the rules so I could know when I was safe — not hurt. In fact, I don't think I have ever known what safe meant. I always wait to see where the hurt will come from this time — where the fear will come from this time. I know that this is not unusual for a child raised in an alcoholic family, but it's really awful."

Judy's big brown eyes sparkled as she continued, "I'm now learning what safe is with my money. I feel safe. Did you hear me? I really feel safe. I have enough money for me — both for my have-to's and for my weekly pleasures.

I am making payments to all my creditors. Oh, it's not as much as they want. But as a responsible, money-managing adult, I didn't ask their permission. In my letter to each of my creditors, I told them — did you hear that? — I *told* them what I could pay them. And I told them when I would be able to make the payment each month, and I promised them that even though I was sending less money than they wanted, I could absolutely promise they would get that amount. I have promised an amount of money I can afford because these are my money rules and I know I can keep them. I haven't made payment commitments that will make me fail. I have set rules and I am able to keep my rules. Good for me!"

Liz's Story

After the congratulations to Judy died down, the room was quiet for a few moments. Then Liz spoke up. "I'm 54 years old. All I have put away for retirement is my basic company retirement. Since my fiftieth birthday, I have worried about retirement. I'm divorced, so there's no one else to rely on. I have to take care of myself. It would be about three in the morning when I would wake up and think about retirement. I would worry, then get a terrible stomachache. I'm considered to be a strong, capable, professional woman. But there in the early morning, I would hold my stomach and cry. I just didn't know what to do. And I was scared. I didn't have any extra money. Or at least I couldn't figure out how to get extra money."

Then a big smile broke across her face as she continued, "Two classes ago, Ruth, you kept encouraging us to 'find a way to make the numbers work' in our budgets. You told us to find a way to pay for what we needed and still make the budget balance. You told us to look both at cutting our expenses and increasing our incomes. Well, I had cut in every way I knew how and still I didn't have the money I needed to put away for retirement. Then I said to myself, in one of my few and far between moments of inspiration in the area of money, 'Why don't I increase my income? Why don't I ask for a raise?'

"Brilliant, right?" Liz continued. "I sat myself down right then before I lost confidence in this brilliant idea of mine. I wrote down all the reasons I felt I had earned an increase in pay. I couldn't believe it, I was asking for a merit raise. The next day I asked a friend to help me organize my writing so it would look more professional. The final paragraph asked for a 10% pay increase for the year. I signed the letter and addressed it to my boss. I also stated in the letter that I would check with him in a couple of days to see if he needed further information. Two days later he called me into his office. I got the raise. Maybe I could've asked for even more. Maybe I will next time.

"But wait," Liz held up her hand when the women started to give her congratulations. "I'm not done yet. The raise was great, but it didn't stop my stomachache in the middle of the night.

"You have to hear this," she continued. "I went directly from my boss's office to the personnel office. At the personnel office I filled out the papers so that the entire — did you hear me — the entire raise went into my 401K retirement plan at work. Not only will my 10% raise go into retirement, but the woman at the personnel office told me the company matches each of my dollars with 25 cents. That means that for every dollar I put in, the company puts in another 25 cents. I'm thrilled. No more stomachaches and tears in the middle of the night. No more fear."

Suzanne's Story

"No more shame for me," Suzanne spoke up. "Let me explain. As part of my divorce settlement, my lawyer asked for and the court granted a monthly maintenance allotment from my former husband. This money — much to the chagrin of my husband — was to allow me to go back to school and get my degree. The degree was to make me more employable. Two months after the divorce was final, my car broke down. I need my car both to get to school and to get to a part-time job I had. The car was going to cost over $400 to fix. I was horrified and scared. I probably made a very big mistake, but I didn't know who else to call, so I called my former husband. I told him I needed help. He told me how irresponsible I was that I had no money to pay for the car repair. He told me how angry he was that I was wasting 'his' money and not saving 'his' money for emergencies such as this. I felt absolutely ashamed. He told me he would send me the money, but he was going to subtract the money he sent me from my next month's maintenance money. He told me to never call him again for money."

Suzanne's voice shook as she continued. "I hung up the phone and I cried. Then I thought of this class and all of you women and I thought of all the difficult financial problems I have heard you solve. And I told myself I was going to do this. I was never going to be in a position to have to be shamed again because of money. Never! Next time there was an emergency, I would have the money. I absolutely would. I took out the expense numbers I had worked with for this class. I was absolutely determined that this time I would make my budget work. I knew it would be hard. But shame was harder. I needed to add more money to my non-monthly emergency expenses so that next time if my old car broke down, I would have the money. In order to do that, I needed more money each month.

"I did two very hard things. I called the place where I worked and asked for more hours, which they were more than happy to give me. I called a college that is about a mile from my house and asked them to put a listing up that I had a room for rent. That was really hard. Two days later, I got a call. I now have a woman roommate. She is very nice and I'm glad for the money. Someday, though, I will have enough money so I don't have to rent a room. Meanwhile the numbers in my budget really work.

"But," Suzanne continued, "there is good news/bad news. Just last week my old car needed a new starter and it needed a tune-up. I was really mad I had to pay more money for that car. That's the bad news. The good news is I had the money in my checkbook. I didn't have to ask anyone for help. I didn't have to feel ashamed. Even though it's hard to work the extra hours and keep up with full-time school. Even though it's hard to share my little house with a roommate, I've found out shame is harder. I've found out I can do this even if it is hard."

Pam's Story

"That's what I've been learning, too," Pam explained to the women in the class. "I've been learning that although it's hard to sit down and pay my bills, I still have to. Instead of saying to myself, 'I can't deal with this. I just can't,' which is what I used to say to myself, I now say, 'Pam, you have to pay those bills. You have to sit down for your business meeting with yourself and pay attention to paying the bills.' I tell myself, just like Suzanne said, 'Paying these bills and following my budget is hard, but shame is harder. It's harder when a creditor calls or my bank calls. That's harder than making my budget work.' So I tell myself, 'Come on, Pam. You can do this money stuff. Anyone who can live with shame for all the years you did can do something like a budget. A budget isn't as hard as shame.'

"That's how I've been talking to myself since we shared in this class about the awful problems we have lived with in our money lives. Ruth, you called them financial consequences. During that class, when I allowed myself to look at how much chaos I had in my money life and how much shame I was living with because of that chaos, I started to tell myself that budgeting had to be easier than shame and chaos. And do you know," Pam continued, "it is. Budgeting is easier. My budget is working! It's really working!"

How Far Have *You* Come?

And now it's *your* turn.

You've made changes and are continuing to make changes in your money life — both in how you think about money and in how you act with your money. I know you've changed because if you hadn't, you wouldn't be reading these words right now. You would have "dropped out" of this book a long time ago. There is no way — absolutely no way — you could have come this far in this book and not grown and changed in your money life.

Open up your notebook that you've been using to record your personal journey of financial empowerment.

Turn back in your notebook to the very first page. Take a few minutes to allow yourself to remember who you were at the beginning of this book.

Read what you wrote about your money training. Read what you wrote about your old, *unworkable* money beliefs. Read what you wrote about your painful, frustrating, *un*workable money behaviors. These are the behaviors that are the result of the old *unworkable* money beliefs.

Are you starting to see how much you have changed as you've read and worked your way through this book?

Now read where you wrote your decision to change. This was your decision that said, "Enough pain. Enough frustration. Enough! No More!" With that decision, whether you really realized it or not, you began the process of change.

Are you reading your new, empowering money beliefs — your affirmations of change? These new beliefs are your new way of thinking about you and your money.

Then you began to learn empowering money skills — new money behaviors. Are you looking at all the work you did to balance your budget and make the numbers work?

Now look at that incredible personal Self-Contract you wrote. This contract contains the new money rules you have set for yourself so that you know — absolutely know — that you are keeping your agreement with yourself to change.

And here you are, almost at the end of this book. You have changed. You have turned your money life around. Like the women in the class, it isn't as if all your money problems are over — far from it. It isn't as if you are, all of a sudden, keeping your money commitment rules perfectly — far from it. It isn't as if you never become discouraged or frustrated — far from it. The biggest way you've changed is that now you *know* you can change the way you think about money, and you *know* you can change the way you behave with your money. You *know* this because you have already changed and you *know* you will continue to change. You, just like the other women in this class, are starting to understand what true empowerment really means. You are starting to understand the vast capacity of your inner strength to make changes even when it is very difficult.

You have changed in your money life. Maybe you've changed in small, quiet ways and maybe you've changed in highly visible ways. But you have changed.

Now it's your turn to talk about how you have changed. It is your turn to talk about what is different in your life, and how your thinking about money has changed and how your money behavior has changed. It is your turn to take a moment and acknowledge your change by writing down in your notebook your response to this question.

"How have I changed both in how I think about my money — my money beliefs — and in how I act with my money — my money behavior? How am I different?"

As you acknowledge the change and growth in your life, know that I and the many, many other women who have worked through this same process of money change and growth offer our congratulations to you.

EPILOGUE

WHAT DO I DO NEXT?

This book has given you, as a woman, both the permission and the tools to change your unworkable money patterns — both in how you think about money and how you act with your money.

Now that you have read and worked through this book, you are forever changed. Whether the changes are only on the inside, or you show these to the outer world, or both, you are different. You are different because you have more knowledge of yourself and you have more knowledge of your use of money.

"What do I do next?" affirms that change is a continual living process of growth. This means you don't want to stop now in your process of money change and growth. I would like to suggest the following eight specific areas for you to pursue further growth in your money life:

1. Go Through This Book Again

Keep using this book as an ongoing text for change. Now would be a great time to begin reading and working through the book all over again. You'll be on a completely different emotional and financial level than when you began this book the first time.

Continue to practice keeping your personal self-contract rules. Just think of all the years you've practiced money the old way. Give yourself time and permission to practice, practice, practice.

2. Get Emotional Support

If you're having trouble letting go of all the old memories and emotions that go with these memories, please get some help. Ask people you trust for a recommendation of a good *therapist*. Then make an appointment and get to work. You don't need to live with the shadows of the past. You can get help in learning to move on in your growth and change.

If you are in a *12-Step recovery group,* your group can be invaluable for getting support in letting go and moving on. If you'd like additional information about 12-Step recovery groups, look under "Alcoholics Anonymous" in the white pages of your local phone book and call the number for information.

3. Build Stashes Of Cash

Keep building "stashes of cash" in your budget. Doesn't that sound wonderful — "stashes of cash?" Your goal is to have enough emergency money saved to be able to pay your bills for at least three months if you are without income. If this money is in your checking account, make sure your checking account earns interest. Ask for information at your *bank*. Or you may want to open a separate savings account or a money market account at your bank for this emergency money. A money market account is simply a savings account that pays a higher interest because you agree to keep a higher amount of money in the account. Again, ask someone at your bank for more information.

Also, if you haven't done this already, get a separate account — a checking account, a savings account or if you don't have enough money *yet,* a bank, jar or sock at home — to save for the pleasures of life that aren't covered by your weekly cash salary. This account will pay for your vacation, your major clothes purchases, major holidays, house furnishings and anything else you consider to be pleasurable.

4. Start Your Retirement Fund Now

Start to save seriously for retirement. You know, each one of us has an aging woman inside of us. Saving money to take care of ourselves when we're older is an important step many women ignore. We can't — absolutely can't — rely on Social Security for enough money to take care of us. Because of death and divorce, women have also found out they can't rely on a man to take care of them either. So we women have to realize that the financial preparation for the aging woman in us is up to us.

Ask women you know for names of *investment advisors*. There are many, many ways to save for your retirement years. It's time to get started saving money for the last third of your life. Ask questions. How are other women saving money for retirement? Then get started.

5. Look Into Your Income Tax Carefully

If you are earning an income, take a look at your tax situation. You may want to check with an *accountant*. Again, ask women you know for names of accountants. You may find ways to save on taxes so you can keep more money for yourself.

If you are self-employed, it is even more important that you get the advice of an accountant. You will want this kind of professional help to make sure you are staying current with estimated taxes and to make sure you have a clear bookkeeping system in your business.

6. Check Into Disability Insurance

Check to see if you have disability insurance. Many times a woman will carry life insurance, which takes care of others when she dies, but the woman doesn't carry disability insurance, which takes care of herself if she becomes ill and can't work.

If you work for a company, check to see if you have disability insurance. If you are self-employed, ask other women for the name of an *insurance agent*. Disability insurance can be expensive, so get more than one cost-quote.

7. Are You In The Right Career?

If you are unhappy in your job *or* you feel you are in a dead-end job *or* you realize you will never earn the money you need to earn in your present job *or* you want to enter the work world, you may want to talk with a *career counselor*. Again, ask others for names of good career counselors in your area.

If you don't want to go to a career counselor, but you would like some information about your interests and personality and where you may fit in the job market, most public universities and vocational schools offer career testing for a fee. Make sure you ask what the fee is, what tests the fee includes and if the fee includes professional test interpretation by one of the staff members.

8. Charitable Contributions For Further Empowerment

As you move further into financial empowerment, you may also want to make a firmer commitment to increased giving. Money is a powerful tool to create change not just in your life, but also in our country and our world.

Women who feel powerless with their money and women who act powerless with their money are not able to reach outside themselves to help others. They are too busy just trying to manage their own lives and survive.

My hope is that as you become financially stronger and more secure, you will make increased giving a part of your budget.

And finally, as I say good-bye to you, I'd like to thank you for the privilege of being your teacher. If you would like to tell me about the growth and change in your money life, you may contact me at this address:

Ruth L. Hayden
P.O. Box 4575
St. Paul, MN 55104

OR, you may contact me in care of my publisher.

♪ APPENDIX

RESOURCES AND BIBLIOGRAPHY

1. Credit Problems

If you are not able to make all your payments to your creditors OR if your creditors are not willing to work with you to lower the amount that you need to pay them each month . . .

Resources

Consumer Credit Counseling is a nonprofit organization that has offices in all major cities in this country. For the telephone number of the office nearest you, look alphabetically in the business section of your telephone white pages or in your telephone yellow pages under "Credit and Debt Counseling Services." The 800 number for Consumer Credit Counseling is 1-800-388-2227.

Many nonprofit social service agencies have professionals on staff called financial counselors. Some of the agencies that may have financial counselors on staff are Lutheran Social Services, Catholic Charities, Jewish Family Services and Family Services. The telephone numbers of these agencies are found alphabetically in the business section of your telephone white pages or in your telephone yellow pages under "Social Service Organizations."

Bibliography

How To Get Out Of Debt by Michael C. Thomsett.

How To Get Out Of Debt, Stay Out Of Debt And Live Prosperously by Jerrold Mundis.

What To Do When The Bill Collector Calls by David J. Kelcher, Jr.

Credit Improvement Handbook by James L. Bandy and Robert A. Freiheit.

2. Bankruptcy

If you believe your financial obligations are beyond your capability to pay and you think you may have to file for bankruptcy . . .

Resources

Contact Consumer Credit Counseling before you make any statements to your creditors or before you see a bankruptcy attorney. See Number 1 in this appendix on how to contact this agency.

Or contact one of the social service agencies listed in Number 1 of this appendix. Set an appointment to talk with a financial counselor at the agency before you see a bankruptcy attorney.

Then if you are advised by a financial counselor that bankruptcy is your best choice, contact a bankruptcy attorney or call Legal Aid/Legal Assistance, which is listed in the business section of your telephone book.

Bibliography

The Bankruptcy Kit by John Ventura.

3. Job Loss

If you have lost your job or have been laid off . . .

Even though you may be angry, resentful, rejected and scared and you may want to just get away as fast as you can from a hurtful situation, do these things before you leave your place of work.

- Check with the personnel office to see if you have any pay owed to you for accrued vacation or sick-day pay.
- Check on the amount and accessibility of the money you have accumulated in retirement contributions.
- Ask for and actually get a completed letter of reference. And make sure it's a good one.
- Ask for help in preparing a resume and ask for job counseling and support. Always ask.
- If there is a severance package agreement, make sure you get a written copy of the severance agreement and actually have in hand the severance checks before you leave the building.

Resources

Ask if your former employer offers any out-placement job assistance.

Most state universities and vocational schools offer career-testing and job-placement services. The number for your local state university or vocational school is found alphabetically in the business section of your telephone book.

Nonprofit, social service agencies usually have a vocational counselor on staff to work with people who have lost their jobs. These agencies and how they can be located are listed in Number 1 of this Appendix.

Your local YWCA may offer vocational and job workshops. You can find the Y's number in the business section of your telephone book.

The federal government has a "Jobs" listing. The federal government's general information number is 1-800-366-2998.

Your city, county and state also have a "Jobs" listing. In the yellow pages of your telephone book, you will find the phone numbers for the city, county and state offices that provide job information.

Bibliography — Jobs

The Government Job Finder by Daniel Lauber.

Jobs '92 by Kathryn and Ross Petra.

Who's Hiring Who: How To Find That Job Fast by Richard Lathrop.

Get The Right Job In 60 Days Or Less by Richard H. Beatty.

Bibliography — Career Change

Wishcraft: How To Get What You Really Want by Barbara Sher.

The 1992 What Color Is Your Parachute? by Richard Nelson Bolles.

4. Starting Your Own Business

If you have decided to become self-employed and want to make sure you develop a financially sound business . . .

Resources

For workshops, training and counseling:
American Women's Economic Development
Corporation (AWED)
60 East 42nd Street, New York, NY 10165
1-800-442-AWED

For "Pre-business" workshops and publications:
Small Business Administration (SBA)
1441 L Street N.W., Washington, DC 20416
1-800-368-5855

You will also find the listing for your local Small Business Administration office in the government pages of your telephone book.

You can get information at this same local number for workshops and counseling that are provided by an organization called S.C.O.R.E. — Service Corps Of Retired Executives. The workshops have a nominal fee. The individual counseling is usually free.

Bibliography

The Competitive Woman by Janet Carmeron.

HERS: The Wise Woman's Guide To Starting A Business On $2,000 Or Less by Carol Milano.

The Start-Up Guide: A One-Year Plan For Entrepreneurs by David H. Bangs, Jr.

How To Run Your Own Home Business by Coralee Smith Kern and Tammara Hoffman Wolfgram.

Invest In Yourself: A Woman's Guide To Starting Her Own Business by Peg Moran.

Your Small Business Made Simple by Richard R. Gallagher, D.B.A.

5. Retirement

If you are realizing you need to plan and save for retirement . . .

Resources

Planning: As part of your retirement planning, you may want to contact Social Security to check on how much money you can expect from Social Security when you retire. The general information number is 1-800-234-5772.

If you are an employee of a company, ask someone in the personnel/benefits department to estimate for you how much retirement money you will receive from the company pension plan, if any, when you retire from the company.

Saving: Whether you have a lot of money or a little, you have the right to be treated with respect by any professional you consult with — whether at a bank or at an investment company. You have the right to ask questions and to have them willingly and clearly answered by the professional. Interview at least two professionals. Then make a decision and pick one of the professionals to work with so you can get started saving money for your retirement years.

Financial planners/investment advisors/financial advisors/investment representatives/stockbrokers — are some of the titles for professionals who work with investments. The best way to get specific names is to ask friends, relatives and colleagues for names of professionals who have done a good job for them by producing a good return on their money *and* who have treated them respectfully.

Bibliography

The 1989/1990 Guide to Social Security Benefits by Leona G. Rubin.

Sylvia Porter's Planning Your Retirement by Sylvia Porter.

Sylvia Porter's Your Finances In The 1990's by Sylvia Porter.

How To Be Your Own Financial Planner by Elliot Raphaelson and Debra Raphaelson West.

6. Bibliography For General Financial Information

Books

The Ms. Money Book by Emily Card, Ph.D.

The Business Of Living by Stephen M. Pollan and Mark Levine.

Making The Most Of Your Money by Jane Bryant Quinn.

Smart Money Moves for the '90s by the Editors of "Money Magazine."

Magazines

"Money Magazine."

"Kiplinger's Personal Finance Magazine."

"Working Woman."